FOUNDATIONS OF RESPONSIVE CAREGIVING

Also by Jean Barbre, EdD

ACTIVITIES FOR RESPONSIVE CAREGIVING: INFANTS, TODDLERS, AND TWOS

Foundations

of
Responsive
Caregiving

Infants,
Toddlers,
and Twos

JEAN BARBRE, EdD

Redleaf Press®
www.redleafpress.org
800-423-8309

Published by Redleaf Press
10 Yorkton Court
St. Paul, MN 55117
www.redleafpress.org

First edition 2013
Cover design by Jim Handrigan
Cover photographs © Ocean Photography/Veer
Interior design by Percolator
Typeset in ITC Stone Serif
Printed in the United States of America

Interior illustration and photographs by Shawn Thomas, except on page 1 © iStockphoto.com/Julie Fairman; page 36 © iStockphoto.com/Michael Reese; pages 39 and 92 © iStockphoto.com/onebluelight; page 75 © iStockphoto.com/Vanessa Morosini; page 77 © iStockphoto.com/Karen Struthers; page 88 © iStockphoto.com /quavondo; page 99 © iStockphoto.com/Christopher Futcher; page 101 © iStockphoto.com/Jo Unruh; and page 115 © iStockphoto.com/Danish Kahn

Library of Congress Cataloging-in-Publication Data
Barbre, Jean.
    Foundations of responsive caregiving : infants, toddlers, and twos / Jean Barbre.
        p. cm.
    Includes bibliographical references and index.
    ISBN 978-1-60554-085-6 (alk. paper)
    1. Child care. 2. Early childhood education. 3. Child development. 4. Parent and infant.
    5. Parent and child.   I. Title.
    HQ778.5.B37 2013
    649'.1—dc23
                                2012025632

Printed on acid-free paper   U17-02

To my husband, Brett:
Thank you for your love and support.

*Too often we underestimate the power of a touch, a smile, a kind word,
a listening ear, an honest compliment, or the smallest act of caring,
all of which have the potential to turn a life around.*
—Leo Buscaglia

Contents

Acknowledgments

I have so many people to thank for supporting me while I wrote this book. First, my husband, for your love and support. For many months, you ignored piles of books on the dining room table, cooked for me, and gave me the time I needed to write. My daughters, Kim and Kat, you're a constant reminder to me of what I can accomplish through hard work and dedication. Your love over the years has made all the difference to me. My mother, brother, and sister, you listened and shared my excitement about writing this book and joyfully shared my accomplishments. My friends, for your generous encouragement and interest in the book. Some of you were there with me from the beginning of this project, and others joined me along the way; I appreciate all of you and treasure your friendship. I especially want to thank my friend Stacy Deeble-Reynolds for allowing me to photograph your home, and my friends and colleagues who allowed me to photograph your beautiful children.

The staff at the Orange Coast College's Harry and Grace Steel Children's Center and the Hatsue Damain Family Child Care Center—you let me photograph your amazing early child care programs. Your commitment to high-quality programs is evident in the smiling faces of the children. A special thanks to Shawn Thomas for your photography and creativity; it was a pleasure to work with you on this book. I thank Doctor Scott Gray, Kim, and Kat for reading the first rough draft of this book and giving me feedback and direction.

The team at Redleaf Press offered me your dedication and hard work. Editors Jeanne Engelmann and Kyra Ostendorf helped make writing this book a pleasure. David Heath at Redleaf offered me early support and the chance to share my thoughts about infants and toddlers with others. The creative team at the press understood what was needed to strengthen the content and flow of the book.

Last, I want to thank the many adults who care for infants and toddlers every day. Your commitment to the care and well-being of our youngest children is commendable. I hope you'll find this book useful and practical, whether you're students going into the field of early care and education or providers who are already caring for children.

To my readers: may you always remember that what you do makes a difference in young children's lives.

Introduction

Those of you who work in early childhood education (ECE) and care programs know they're noisy, exciting places. Children from birth to age three are bundles of energy whose bodies are in constant motion. Infants, toddlers, and twos can sweep from frustration to joy, delight, and tears within minutes. They love to cuddle, listen to stories, and sleep gently in your arms. It's easy for babies to melt your heart when they look up at you with their big toothless grins. You know there's nothing quite as sweet or precious as a young child. They captivate and motivate you—their wonderment and delight make your work rewarding even when you're tired. Their innocence and sense of wonder bring you joy and hope, and they inspire you to provide them with the highest-possible quality of care.

The care that infants, toddlers, and twos receive dramatically affects their future intellectual, social, emotional, and physical development. And you play a critical role in determining if they will acquire the skills they need to succeed in life. As if this wasn't already an overwhelming amount of responsibility, remember too that the relationships you build with young children are going to affect their ability to form healthy relationships for the rest of their lives.

CARING FOR CHILDREN

The term *caregiver* typically refers to any adult besides the parent or guardian who cares for a child for any length of time. But you don't want to be just *any* caregiver—you want to be a *responsive* caregiver, and that means you actively create nurturing relationships with the children you care for. These very young humans are almost wholly dependent on you for their physical, mental, and emotional well-being, and they need you to respond to their needs quickly and in developmentally appropriate ways.

What else characterizes you as a responsive caregiver? You plan activities that help children learn the skills they need to develop across the domains of social-emotional, physical, cognitive, and language development. You take advantage of unplanned opportunities—what are called *teachable moments*—to help children learn new things and build on existing knowledge. You create environments in which they can safely and joyfully explore, discover, and create their own meaning.

THE IMPORTANCE OF RELATIONSHIPS

During infancy and toddlerhood, children learn almost everything through their relationships. They interact and observe other children and adults. To be an effective ECE professional, you need to understand more about the healthy relationships that are cornerstones to children's emotional well-being. (I discuss this further in chapter 3.) You need specific skills and knowledge so you can provide optimal care for each and every child.

High-quality ECE programs hire highly qualified caregivers and adhere to the best practices of child development. You should be knowledgeable about early development and understand its importance in the development of infants, toddlers, and twos. With such knowledge, you can provide the care and nurturing that very young children need. It's through the relationships you build and the trusting environment you provide that children can learn and build trust.

Young children are cared for in a variety of settings: at home, where they are cared for by family members; in nonlicensed care in the homes of relatives, friends, or neighbors; in licensed ECE centers or licensed family child care homes. (In chapter 1, I describe the different kinds of care and the indicators of high-quality programs.) I call the settings that licensed ECE centers and family child care homes provide *early care and learning environments*. You can adapt the information I provide to any setting where you offer early care to infants, toddlers, and twos.

For ease of reading, I use the terms *caregiver* and *responsive caregiver* interchangeably. I'm assuming that you are striving to be a responsive caregiver (or perhaps you are one already). You teach and care for children and attend to their individual needs in warm, nurturing, loving ways. Your interactions with children are positive

and respectful, and you are genuinely interested in their well-being. You honor the children's diversity by supporting their home languages and cultural backgrounds. (I discuss these practices in chapter 2 and in the closing thoughts at the end of the book.) You enjoy caring for children and provide uncountable moments of nurturing and developmentally appropriate learning experiences.

Six principles are woven throughout this book:

1. Responsive caregiving is essential to children's growth and development.

2. Trust is the cornerstone of healthy relationships.

3. Children need stable, secure early care and learning environments.

4. Children are ready and eager to learn.

5. Play is central to children's learning.

6. Responsive caregivers collaborate with families to support children's growth and development.

As a professional, you have been entrusted with the care of vulnerable young children. You need knowledge of ECE, experience in caring for young children, a commitment to excellence, and ongoing professional development. You also need to know how to create and sustain environments in which children can grow across the developmental domains. Children grow best when they are loved, cared for, and valued as unique individuals. They need your whole-hearted love and commitment to help them reach their full potential.

ABOUT THIS BOOK

I wrote *Foundations of Responsive Caregiving* to help you become a responsive care-giver. I'm going to acquaint you with theories of child development, components of high-quality care, best practices in teaching and caregiving, and an overview of how children grow and develop from birth to age three. I also provide you with strategies for supporting children who have special needs.

Each chapter offers tips on how to promote young children's learning, a summary of the big ideas to take away from that chapter, and reflection and application questions to help you explore the ideas further. Chapters 6, 7, 8, and 9 address the four learning domains. In each of those chapters, you'll find references to my companion book, *Activities for Responsive Caregiving*. The activities in that book can help you implement age-appropriate activities and strategies through play.

But before you look at these many elements of responsive care, you need to first explore your personal caregiving philosophy.

EXPLORING YOUR PERSONAL CAREGIVING PHILOSOPHY

Creating your personal caregiving philosophy statement requires you to think about what you know and feel about working with young children. This important state-ment can help you reflect on your current beliefs and attitudes and deepen your commitment to caring for young children. You might include your core beliefs 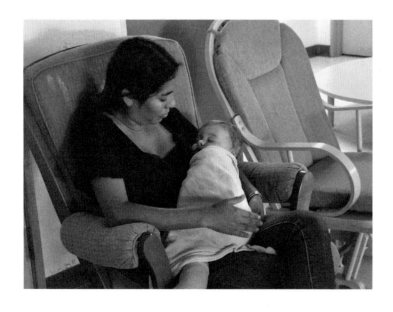 about caring for infants, toddlers, and twos; your approach to teaching and caring for other people; and your com-mitment to quality care for all children. Make your statement personal, and use it to inspire and motivate you to become the best caregiver you can.

Start by asking yourself, *What can I do to ensure that children reach their full po-tential and grow to be emotionally healthy?* Next, reflect on who you are as a teacher and caregiver. What skills do you bring to those roles? What areas do you think need strengthening? Are some areas more challenging to you than others? Assess the areas you see as your strengths and those you feel need improving. Because everyone can improve on her skills and expertise, examine what you're doing right now to increase your knowledge of child development.

Creating your personal caregiving philosophy statement can help you focus on why you entered the field of ECE, what joys and concerns you have now, what your gifts are as a caregiver, and how to deepen your commitment to young children. The field of ECE changes continually. Don't allow yourself to get stale! Keep taking classes and workshops to improve your teaching practices, try new things, and acquire new ideas. Learning also reminds you why you chose to work with young children in the first place.

Personal Caregiving Philosophy Statement

Complete the following statements:

1. I entered the field of child development because _____.

2. The most rewarding part of my job is _____.

3. My greatest concern for the children I care for is _____.

4. My greatest gift is _____.

5. I am committed to _____.

Here's a sampling of responses:

1. I entered the field of child development because *I care about the well-being of young children.*

2. The most rewarding part of my job is *seeing the smiling faces of the children each day and watching them grow and discover the world.*

3. My greatest concern for the children I care for is *that they won't have an opportunity just to be children and that they will grow up too fast.*

4. My greatest gift is *my ability to nurture young children.*

5. I am committed to *giving children 100 percent of my love and attention each day.*

What do these completed statements have in common? Try to identify the elements that are similar in each of them; these are the strengths and motivators of the caregiver who wrote this statement. Pay attention to similarities in your own statements. You might also look for statements that are *not* congruent, that don't seem to fit with the rest. Perhaps these represent new interests or ones that you've kept buried. It's important to give careful consideration to each statement.

After you've completed your statement and thought it over, post it in a prominent place, like your entryway or welcome space, so you and the children's parents can see it daily. If you write your statement at a staff meeting, share it with your coworkers and the larger school community.

FINAL THOUGHTS
. . . .

Young children grow and develop best in loving, stable, nurturing environments. Help them develop their foundations for future learning and healthy, stable relationships. In a high-quality early care setting, you can create opportunities for children to learn while you protect and care for them. You can explore who you are as a caregiver and use your new understanding to help children learn. You chose to become a highly qualified ECE professional, and that means having an ongoing commitment to professional development and program excellence.

To help you achieve your goals, in the next chapter I discuss varieties of child care, characteristics of infants and toddlers, and your role as a caregiver.

WHAT CAREGIVERS CAN DO

- Respond to the needs of the whole child.
- Respond to infants, toddlers, and twos in a warm, nurturing, loving manner.
- Demonstrate a genuine interest in children's well-being.
- Increase your knowledge of child development.
- Explore your commitment to infants and toddlers.
- Create a personal caregiving philosophy statement.
- Share your statement with families and coworkers.
- Use your statement to set personal goals that expand and deepen your skills and commitment to very young children.

BIG IDEAS FOR CAREGIVERS

- Caregivers need specific knowledge and skills so they can provide optimal early care and learning environments.
- Caregivers teach and guide children's learning.
- Children grow best where they are loved, cared for, and valued as unique individuals.

REFLECTION AND APPLICATION

1. Identify three teachable moments you've experienced. How did you use those moments to build on a child's learning?

2. Name three ways you can improve yourself as a caregiver.

3. Apply your personal caregiving philosophy statement to your work with young children. Do your actions and statement align? Why or why not?

4. What two things can you do to further your commitment to ECE?

Caregiving and the Early Childhood Professional

As an early childhood professional who cares for infants, toddlers, and twos, you play a critical role in children's growth and development. You are essential to their well-being and future development, and this takes commitment and dedication. You need to know what responsive caregiving is, the types of care available, and the developmental stages of infants, toddlers, and twos. Such knowledge deepens your understanding and improves the quality of care you provide.

CHARACTERISTICS OF RESPONSIVE CAREGIVERS

As a responsive caregiver, you do a lot! To make a long story short, you provide a loving, nurturing, stable, and responsive learning environment for all children. You respond to their needs quickly and appropriately. Because infants and toddlers are wholly dependent on adults for their care and safety, their well-being lies in your hands.

Positive interactions with caregivers are critical to children's formation of early attachment and trust. You create an atmosphere in which these can arise: Your setting is relaxed and peaceful. You recognize that establishing trust with the important adults in their lives is the cornerstone for how children will feel about themselves and others throughout their lives. As children develop and change, you modify your program to meet their changing needs.

You continuously evaluate your activities, the environment you've created, and the children in your care. You're flexible in your daily schedule, balancing the predictability and comfort of routines with the changing needs of children. You adjust and modify your setting so children can master their developmental milestones. Because a cohort of children differs so widely, you plan a range of activities that vary in difficulty. You challenge children, but only to the extent that they can successfully master new skills with some effort. For example, a toddler may play initially with a wooden puzzle that has four pieces, each with a giant knob on it. You might then offer him a more challenging puzzle that lacks knobs, so he must grab and lift the puzzle pieces with his fingers. As the child masters these skills, you continue to offer him greater complexity, greater challenges—perhaps a puzzle with more pieces. In other words, you plan rich, stimulating experiences so children can explore and learn at their own developmental pace.

You also follow children's interests so their activities remain child directed. Your focus is on encouraging infants, toddlers, and twos to discover and explore their world freely. You offer them activities that stimulate growth across the social-emotional, physical, cognitive, and language development domains. (My companion book, *Activities for Responsive Caregiving: Infants, Toddlers, and Twos*, provides 101 play-based activities you can use in your program to foster such growth.)

Here, in checklist form, are the essential qualities of responsive caregivers:

✔ Caring

✔ Nurturing

✔ Knowledgeable

✔ Patient

✔ Reliable

✔ Consistent

✔ Flexible

✔ Humorous

More and more children are spending the majority of their days (and some of their nights) in the care of adults other than family members, and they must receive quality care. Children deserve to be cared for by knowledgeable, nurturing, caring, and responsive individuals. Such care can be provided in a variety of settings. One or another of these may suit them best.

TYPES OF CHILD CARE

There are two main types of licensed care for infants, toddlers, and twos: family child care and center-based care. Whatever the organizational model, child care programs need adults committed to quality care. In the highest-quality programs, caregivers implement known best practices:

- **Licensed family child care homes** Licensing requirements for family child care vary from state to state. Usually in-home providers can care for only a small group of children at a time. Family child care offers families flexible hours and is usually the most affordable. Children are cared for in homey settings where they can interact and learn together. Depending on the number of children in the home, care may be provided by one adult or by an adult and

an assistant. It's not uncommon for infants, toddlers, preschoolers, and even schoolagers to be cared for in the same family home. Children in such settings often remain in the same family child care home for several years, giving them the benefit of a primary caregiver and continuity of care during their formative years. The National Association for Family Child Care (NAFCC) and family child care associations in many states offer providers resources and professional development training to improve the quality of their programs.

- **Licensed early care centers** These centers provide more standardized and regulated care. Although requirements differ from state to state, licensing usually regulates adult-to-child ratios, group size, hours of operation, teaching practices, teacher qualifications, and health and safety standards. Several models exist: for-profit, nonprofit, state or federally funded, and private corporation-owned or -sponsored.

BEST PRACTICES IN CHILD CARE

Best practices in early childhood education (ECE) encourage growth of the whole child in all four developmental domains. (Chapters 6 through 9 provide information on each domain and discuss how to promote their development in caregiving settings.) High-quality ECE settings employ teachers who are nurturing, caring, and knowledgeable about child development. There's no one indicator of quality infant and toddler care. These are the indicators that are widely recognized in the field of ECE:

- Ongoing, nurturing relationships are cultivated between children and responsive caregivers.

- Environments are physically safe.

- Children are assigned a primary caregiver.

- Children's individual needs are respected.

- Activities promote children's learning.

- Schedules and routines meet the individual needs of children, including those with special needs.

- Caregivers form successful partnerships with parents.

- Experiences are structured so children can build and practice skills across the developmental domains.

- Children are offered age-appropriate choices.

- Children's learning opportunities are built upon existing knowledge.

- Children learn in a play-based environment.

Leading ECE organizations help caregivers identify best practices. The National Association for the Education of Young Children (NAEYC) has adopted position statements on quality ECE. These organizations support high-quality early care and education by promoting program standards, developmentally appropriate practices, partnerships with families, and highly qualified, knowledgeable teachers. NAEYC provides parents and early childhood educators with resources and information. You can learn more about its services and read its current position statements at www .naeyc.org.

The Program for Infant/Toddler Care (PITC) is cosponsored by the California Department of Education and WestEd, a nonprofit organization that promotes research, evaluation, and professional development to improve education and human development. PITC supports high-quality programs by providing parents and caregivers with standards of care. Its mission is to ensure that infants and toddlers receive safe, emotionally and intellectually rich care. Like NAEYC, PITC offers recommendations covering six programs for infants and toddlers: primary care, small groups, individualized care, continuity, cultural responsiveness, and inclusion of children with special needs (PITC, accessed 2012). The PITC website is www.pitc.org.

Primary Care

Primary care is a best practice widely recognized in child care. It includes feeding, changing diapers, rocking, soothing, talking, and engaging the child. Each child should be assigned one primary caregiver. Primary caregivers are assigned several children to care for, based on the ratio of adults to children in their program. Although they interact with all children in the setting, primary caregivers' main responsibility is to provide the primary, personalized care for their assigned children.

Those with whom children spend considerable time but who are not the primary caregiver are termed *secondary caregivers*. Primary caregivers coordinate the care offered by these other professionals so that children are treated consistently. Primary caregivers must communicate effectively with the rest of the caregiving team so all children receive optimal care and reach their next developmental milestones.

When young children reach designated milestones or specific ages, they are typically promoted to the next level of care. Many centers, however, are starting to embrace the concept *continuity of care*, in which children remain together as a cohort.

This practice allows children and primary caregivers to move together to the next level of care. Typically, centers offer three levels of care for children under age three: infant, toddler, and two-year-old care. When children turn three, they usually move to a new classroom structured to meet their new needs and skills. Continuity of care benefits children under age three in the following ways:

- It supports relationship building by strengthening children's attachment to their primary caregivers.

- It builds trusting relationships between peers, allowing caregivers to focus on building children's developing skills.

- It maintains continuing relationships between families and caregivers.

Communication between Home and Care Program

Another critical component of high-quality programs is effective communication between children's homes and the early care program. (I discuss partnerships between parents and caregivers further in the closing thoughts at the end of the book.) Respecting each family's cultural beliefs and providing children with a safe, bias-free environment helps children feel valued and respected. (I examine how cultures influence the social-emotional development of young children in chapter 6.) When parents and caregivers work well together, their efforts help children grow and develop to their full potential.

Low Adult-to-Child Ratios

High-quality family child care and center-based programs offer children the care and attention they need. The youngest children need a higher adult-to-child ratio than older children. Although such care costs families more, the lower ratios are needed because of the intensity of caring for the youngest children. NAEYC (2008) recommends that the adult-to-child ratio vary with group size and age of children. According to NAEYC, quality care requires a 1:3 or 1:4 adult-to-infant (birth–12 months) ratio, a 1:4 or 1:5 adult-to-toddler (12–28 months) ratio, and a 1:5 or 1:6 adult-to-twos (21–36 months) ratio. Small groups and individualized care offer young children the chance to build healthy relationships with caregivers and other children. Individualized and continuous care also gives them chances to build on their existing strengths and knowledge.

CARING FOR INFANTS, TODDLERS, AND TWOS

Deciding which age group to care for is an important decision for you. You need to think about which age group and learning environment suit you best. Understanding each age group and stage will help you make your choice. Both caring and teaching are integral to your role, and in each, you need to be able to put the needs of children ahead of your own.

Caregivers for infants, toddlers, and twos genuinely care about the health and well-being of the youngest children. Typically, those of you who care for this age group love what you do. You prefer children in this age range, and your preferences may be even more particular; for example, you may like caring for infants but not enjoy working with toddlers and two-year-olds.

Infants need continuous care, monitoring, holding, and comforting. Those of you who work with them typically love babies. And that's fortunate because infants can be demanding! You need to enjoy responding to their immediate needs, including feeding, changing their diapers, and providing safe, comforting places for them to grow and develop. Toddler learning environments are very different: they are busy, often noisy, places where children spend a lot of time on the floor. Toddlers are learning to move and explore the world, and they sometimes demonstrate their newfound independence through challenging behaviors. The two-year-old classroom is also busy, noisy, and exciting. Twos walk, run, and engage in pretend play. They enjoy singing, playing with and on musical instruments, and being read to by adults. Their growing ability to talk and ask questions fuels their drive to learn about the world. Providing optimal care to this age group takes special knowledge, expertise—and energy.

Some caregivers move from teaching preschool to providing infant-toddler care. If you're making such a move, remember that your new responsibilities will be quite different from those of preschool teachers. Most preschool children are already potty trained or are learning to manage their toileting routines. They have usually mastered skills like dressing and undressing themselves, asking simple questions, and communicating their needs with words. Infants and toddlers, on the other hand, still depend on adults to provide their basic needs. While you're tending to their basic needs, you must also support their learning across the developmental domains.

Programs that adhere to best practices provide consistent routines and schedules to give children a sense of predictability, which they need to develop trust and security. (I discuss the important of routines further in chapter 5.) A large part of caring for very young children is creating opportunities for them to experience the world firsthand and to become more independent. Through uncountable interactions, you teach infants, toddlers, and twos the fundamentals of language, navigating the world, and forming relationships and acquiring independence and a sense of self. To achieve these aims, you must be patient, nurturing, and responsive to every child in your care.

CHARACTERISTICS OF INFANTS, TODDLERS, AND TWOS

Children from birth to age three typically exhibit a series of developmental milestones. Because each of them grows at a different pace, you'll see children who master skills much earlier or later than others. One child may walk at twelve months, while another is just starting to do so at fourteen months. Knowing the developmental characteristics of very young children is essential so you can help meet their needs through meaningful play and other activities.

High-quality ECE offers learning opportunities to all children with few restrictions. In the least-restrictive environment, children can participate in all activities and use all materials and indoor and outdoor spaces. Such an environment offers children developmentally appropriate learning opportunities. Doing so is particularly important because early intervention is critical to early brain development. Children with developmental delays need chances to reach their developmental milestones. (I discuss the importance of early interventions further in chapters 4 and 5.)

You know that children reach their developmental milestones at different rates. Some move easily along the continuum in a textbook-like progression. Others move more slowly toward mastery, while still others experience developmental delays that require special intervention. For example, one infant might begin cooing sounds like *aaaaaaa*, *ooooooo*, and *eeeeeee* and begin gurgling at three months. Another child might make babbling sounds like *dada* and *gaga* at four months. Because such a wide range of mastery exists, early childhood professionals define the ages and stages for children from birth to age three in various ways. In this book, I identify children as young infants (birth to six months), older infants (six to twelve months), young toddlers (twelve to twenty-four months), and older toddlers/twos (twenty-four to thirty-six months). Certain developmental characteristics within these age ranges are common:

Characteristics of Children from Birth to Age Three

AGE	CHARACTERISTICS	
Young infant: Birth to six months	• Vocalizes, including cooing, babbling, gurgling, and laughing • Smiles and imitates adults' facial expressions • Raises chest and head while lying on stomach • Reaches for hanging objects with hands • Watches faces and follows moving objects	• Turns head toward sounds • Shows social smiles directed to other people • Laughs and smiles in response to active stimulation • Enjoys social play and shows a special relationship with caregivers • Grasps and shakes hand toys • Explores books with mouth and hands

Characteristics of Children from Birth to Age Three (cont'd)

AGE	CHARACTERISTICS	
Older infant: Six to twelve months	• Uses vocal sounds to express joy and displeasure • Repeats babbling sounds • Begins to respond to "no" • Rolls over easily • Sits with, and later without, support • Reaches with one hand and passes objects from hand to hand • Crawls and creeps on hands and knees	• Pulls self to standing position with assistance • Finds partially hidden objects and explores them with hands and mouth • Enjoys smiling and laughing • Demonstrates playful engagement with caregivers by reaching for and seeking them out to play • Can show distress and wariness around strangers
Young toddler: Twelve to twenty-four months	• Tries to imitate words and responds to simple verbal commands • Responds to and shakes head to gesture "no" • Uses two- to four-word sentences and follows simple directions • Begins to walk and to push and pull toys • Kicks a large ball and climbs up and down furniture and stairs with assistance	• Places two to three cubes or small blocks on top of each other • Turns the pages of books • Becomes aware of self as separate from others and demonstrates increased independence • Shows first signs of empathy, embarrassment, and pride
Older toddler/ two-year-old: Twenty-four to thirty-six months	• Uses four- to five-word sentences • Language more understandable and grammatically correct • Understands and recognizes common objects and pictures • Sorts objects by shape and size • Matches pictures to objects • Uses crayon to draw strokes on paper • Walks and runs with ease and can pedal a tricycle	• Can say own name, age, and sex • Engages in pretend play and can take turns with peers • Understands concepts of *me, mine,* and *his/hers* • Imitates others and is aware of self as separate from others • Show signs of pride, embarrassment, and self-consciousness

FINAL THOUGHTS

Choosing to care for very young children is an important decision. As a responsive caregiver, you play a critical role in providing children with optimal learning opportunities. Best practices recommend that care be provided by nurturing, caring, and knowledgeable professionals. The program you work in provides quality care by promoting children's development in all domains. It focuses on best practices and strives to meet individual children's needs. You and your program offer developmentally appropriate activities to support the growth and development of the whole child.

WHAT CAREGIVERS CAN DO

- Support families while they make the move into the early care setting.
- Provide responsive primary care to infants and toddlers.
- Respect the needs of all children, including those with special needs.
- Ensure that your program meets health and safety standards.
- Design programs that are developmentally appropriate.
- Maintain small group size and low adult-to-child ratios.
- Plan child-directed activities.
- Acquire knowledge about early child development.

. . . .

BIG IDEAS FOR CAREGIVERS

- Young children are assigned a primary caregiver.
- Continuity of care offers children the chance to form strong attachments.
- Meet children's needs individually.

. . . .

REFLECTION AND APPLICATION

1. How can you increase your knowledge of infants, toddlers, and twos?
2. What are the benefits of continuity of care for infants and toddlers?
3. Name five things you can do to provide a nurturing and caring environment for all children.
4. What are three best practices you can apply to your work with young children?

Theory
to Practice

Best practices in early childhood education (ECE) and care are grounded in theories of child development. These theories have their roots in thinkers like seventeenth-century philosopher John Locke and continue to deepen in the work of contemporaries like T. Berry Brazelton and Stanley Greenspan. Locke suggested that the child's mind is a *tabula rasa* (Latin for "blank slate")—a vacuum at birth that life filled up (Berk 2008). Locke believed that what we now call *nurture* accounts for what humans learn and become. He recognized the value of caring, nurturing environments because they prepared unformed, blank humans to better learn about their worlds. Since the seventeenth century, many educators, philosophers, medical professionals, and others have contributed to the fields of child development and ECE. Today, we know that infants are born ready to learn and already endowed with brains wired to build relationships, seek information, learn language, and discover the world.

PSYCHOSOCIAL THEORY

One of the best-known researchers and theorists in child development is Erik Erikson (1902–94). As a disciple of Sigmund Freud, Erikson studied how people's culture and life events influence their development. Erikson identified eight stages of human development, during which individuals must resolve eight fundamental conflicts (one for each stage). Those that are pertinent to your work with infants, toddlers, and twos are stages 1 (birth to one year) and 2 (one to three years).

Erikson believed that individuals develop and resolve these conflicts throughout their lives. His important contribution to the field of ECE is his conviction of the peculiar challenge of infants and toddlers to develop feelings of trust and autonomy.

Erikson's (1963) Eight Stages of Psychosocial Development

PSYCHOSOCIAL STAGE	AGE	NEW DIMENSION
Basic trust versus mistrust	Birth to twelve months	To develop feelings of trust and a sense that the world is safe
Autonomy versus shame and doubt	Age one to age three	To develop feelings of self-sufficiency and confidence in the ability to do things alone
Initiative versus guilt	Age three to age six	To expand the desire to explore and initiate new things and develop a sense of purpose
Industry versus inferiority	Age six to age eleven	To expand the capacity to cooperate with others and develop basic skills
Identity versus role confusion	Adolescence	To answer the question "Who am I in the world?" and explore personal values and beliefs about self
Intimacy versus isolation	Young adulthood	To form an intimate, lasting, and loving relationship with another person
Generativity versus stagnation	Middle age	To contribute to the next generation, through child rearing and caring for other people or through other productive work and accomplishments
Ego integrity versus despair	Late life	To enjoy grandchildren and reflect on one's life as worthwhile

Trust versus Mistrust

Although Erikson's psychoanalytic concepts continue to be examined and challenged, his views on the formation of trust and the building of autonomy remain important and relevant to our field. He identified the first stage in human life as one in which the child wrestles with trust and mistrust. Erikson believed that infants need to resolve the conflict between wariness (mistrust) and feeling confident about the adults around them (trust) (Patterson 2009). He observed that infants and toddlers build trust when they receive warm and responsive care (Berk 2008).

The role of adult caregivers in the infant's formation of trust is critical because it's the caregiver who ensures that the relationship with the infant is in fact trustworthy. Trust is now considered the foundation of all healthy relationships. In trusting relationships, people feel physically, emotionally, and psychologically safe. When they experience these feelings, they can grow into authentic human beings. Without trust, people's relationships lack a solid foundation and individuals feel inauthentic and weakly attached to others.

Erikson speculated that mistrust becomes established when infants experience prolonged periods of tension: their needs are not met, they experience long periods of discomfort, or they are treated harshly (Berk 2008). According to Erikson, in these situations infants internalize the world as not good. They experience this non-goodness by transferring it to themselves: *they* are not good, good enough, or worthy. Such internalization occurs unconsciously, at a very primitive level of children's developing sense of self. Unhappily, these feelings become central to how children see themselves in the world.

When children who have experienced feelings of mistrust move toward the next developmental stage that Erikson identified (autonomy), they do so with feelings of shame and doubt. Mistrust, Erikson believed, erodes children's feelings of self-confidence and self-worth. In mistrustful relationships with parents and caregivers, these children are less likely to experience authentic feelings of self-worth and are more likely to interact unhealthily with adults and peers.

Caregivers who respond to children in nurturing, loving ways set the stage for them to develop a strong sense of trust. You respond to children regardless of their happiness or irritability, their health or sickness, their laughter or crying. You love and care for them unconditionally. You respond tenderly when they cry because their diapers are wet. Your reactions are immediate and helpful, and because you are tender with them, children begin to build trust in you.

Young children learn how to regulate their emotions when you guide them into closer relationships with you, other adults, and peers. For example, if a toddler hits another child, you try to comfort and ensure the safety of both children. You say calmly, "We don't hit," and you gently redirect both children in a caring way. It's important that you respond verbally and nonverbally, because young children are aware of both forms of communication. Your tone of voice, your touch, and your body language tell them as much as your words. The trust-building sequence I outline here (figure 2.1) describes how trust is formed between an early childhood professional or parent and a child.

Figure 2.1 Trust-Building Sequence

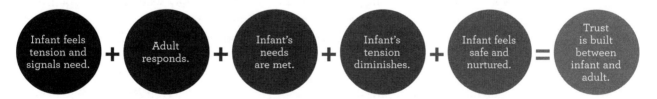

The trust-building sequence begins when a child first feels tension. This may be because she is hungry, wet, tired, understimulated, or overstimulated. The child may experience tension because she wants to be held or comforted. In any of these cases, she will try to signal her need by smiling or gurgling, wiggling her legs or arms, or moving her head. She may also begin to cry, because crying is an effective way for an infant to communicate her needs to an adult. Those of you who work with young children know that every child has a unique set of cries. Caregivers can create a trusting environment by responding appropriately to a child's cries. Trust is formed when her needs are met and her feelings of tension and discomfort diminish. Positive interactions build trust between you and the child.

The formation of mistrust is more complex. Here, the child's tension and distress become intensified by the lack of response or the inadequate response from the caregiver. Like the trust-building sequence (figure 2.1), the mistrust sequence begins when a child feels tension and exhibits it. The adult may acknowledge the child's efforts to communicate through crying but does nothing to eliminate the child's source of tension. For example, a child may cry because he is hungry. An unresponsive adult may acknowledge the child's cries but does not immediately feed him. In other words, the unresponsive caregiver does not relieve the child's discomfort; the child's cry for help is ignored.

Crying is one of the few ways in which very young children can communicate their needs. Typically, as they continue to cry, their cries becoming louder and more intense until their needs are met or they give up signaling their distress. Throughout this escalation of tension, their bodies become increasingly tense and stiff. An adult can choose to respond or continue to ignore them. Nonresponsive gestures or delayed responses only serve to reinforced children's growing tension and distress. During periods of high tension like these, children begin to internalize the world as a not-good, untrustworthy place. They move toward feelings of mistrust.

Children in states of high tension cry a lot and are difficult to comfort or console. Unhappily, it's easy for adults to distance themselves emotionally from seemingly inconsolable infants. You've undoubtedly heard people say, "Leave him alone; just let him cry it out" or "Don't pick her up; she's just a fussy baby." Allowing infants a few minutes to cry or fuss won't harm them, but repeated long periods of crying and being ignored or left alone puts children at risk.

Knowing the children in your care and their different cries are important components of responsive caregiving. It's easy to see in the mistrust-building sequence (figure 2.2) why children's distress behaviors become increasingly challenging for adults: caring for crying children increases *your* stress. If the high-tension state repeats itself, the child's feelings of mistrust, shame, and doubt increase. The child learns that the world is not a safe, loving place. Is it any wonder she may seem inconsolable?

The trust-building and mistrust-building sequences occur among parents, caregivers, and children. Always remember that children who come into your program may live in homes where their primary needs are not being met or are not met well. If you suspect that parents are neglecting their children and that the children's health and safety are at risk, you must take appropriate action. Neglected children may exhibit symptoms of failure to thrive, such as a lack of interest in their surroundings and a failure to grow, gain weight, or reach developmental milestones. In cases of extreme neglect, intervention is essential to protect the children's physical health and safety. Share your concerns with the appropriate person, and if necessary, follow your center's policies for reporting child abuse and neglect.

Advocating for children is one of your responsibilities as a caregiver. You can build trusting relationships with infants through the following activities:

- rocking and soothing a crying baby

- responding to the infant's attention-seeking signals

- engaging in eye-to-eye contact with an infant

Figure 2.2: Mistrust-Building Sequence

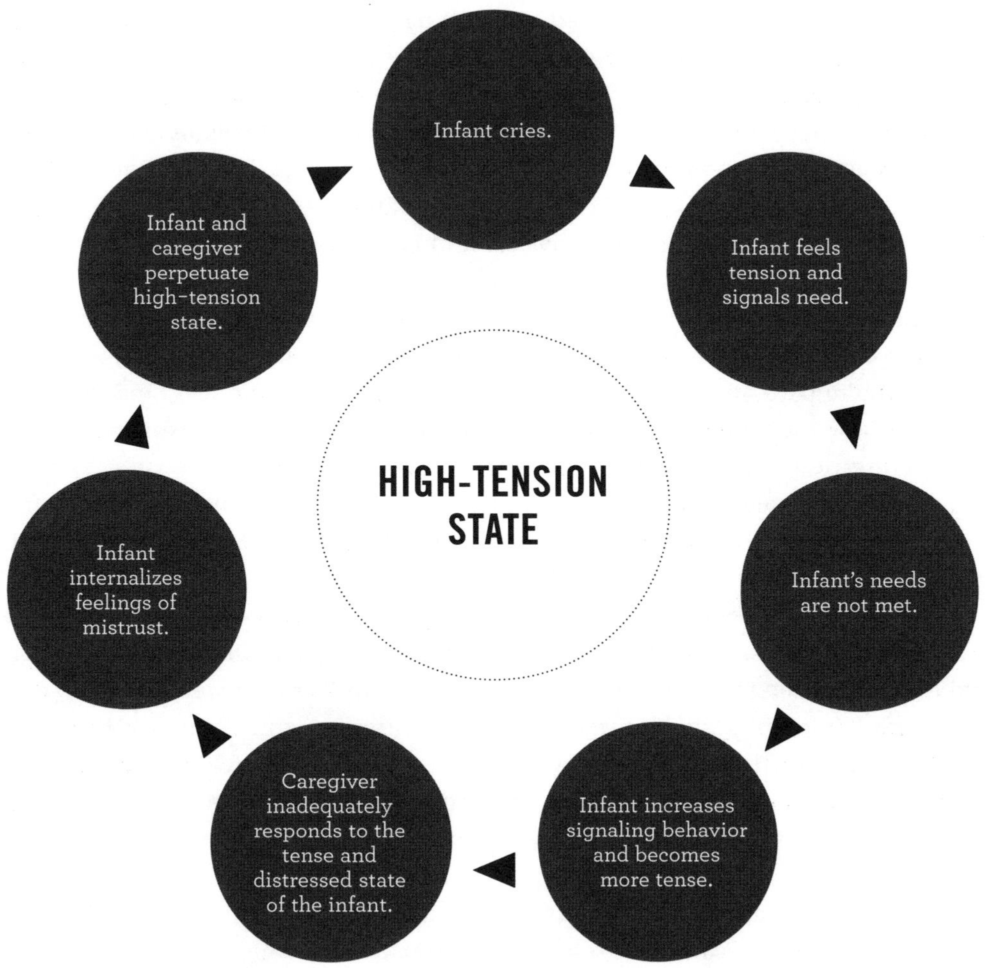

- smiling reciprocally

- touching an infant gently while feeding or changing his diaper

- reading and talking to the child throughout the day

- being aware of your own body posture, touch, and tone of voice

Autonomy versus Shame and Doubt

Erikson believed that each of his eight stages of development built on the previous one. Infants must develop trust before they can become autonomous toddlers. When children reach their first birthdays, they begin to exhibit Erikson's second stage of development. The goal of this stage is to develop feelings of autonomy rather than feelings of shame and doubt. Autonomous children become increasingly more self-sufficient and confident in their ability to do things alone.

The cognitive abilities of children between ages one and three increase rapidly. Their developing gross-motor and fine-motor skills urge them to explore the world enthusiastically; their new mobility and dexterity help them push and pull wheeled toys and to climb, run, and jump. Their newly honed fine-motor skills allow them to begin dressing themselves and to use crayons and playdough. At this point, children start exhibiting *me do*, *mine*, and *I can do it myself* attitudes. Building on their foundation of trust and their growing physical and cognitive skills, they become more independent and autonomous.

You play an important role in fostering children's growing feelings of autonomy. In high-quality care, children's efforts to try new things are encouraged and supported. You're patient with their efforts to do things for themselves, and you give them the time they need to practice their developing skills, such as using utensils to feed themselves, putting on coats or sweaters, and deciding which toys to play with. You modify your care to promote their independence. For example, you might offer toddlers and twos a no-splash pitcher so they can pour their own milk easily, with minimal spills.

At the same time, you balance their emerging autonomy with limits that ensure their safety and sense of security. Toddlers and twos have a limited sense of what is and isn't safe. Therefore, it's important that you set limits to ensure their safety and well-being. Unhappily, this can mean that they often may hear the word *no* from you. You can help them learn what they can and cannot do safely in a loving, caring way. Be a comforting and patient presence when they become frustrated. Avoid negative responses to behavior, including "You're a bad girl" or "That was a very bad thing to do."

Children internalize adults' negative responses and develop feelings of shame and self-doubt; these can lead to a negative sense of self and a hesitation to try

new things, lest they be punished for doing so. Children who internalize "I'm not good enough," "I'm bad," and "I'm too afraid to try something new" don't develop a healthy sense of self. (I discuss social-emotional development in detail in chapter 6.)

Carefully observe the children you care for and foster their feelings of autonomy. Be purposeful in supporting and encouraging any children who display feelings of shame and self-doubt. If you spot such feelings in the children you care for, you must become more intentional in your own responses and interactions with them. Often adults will work with children to diminish feelings of shame and doubt simply by saying, "You're such a good

girl!" or "I really like how you painted the picture." Unfortunately, praise alone is not enough to enable children to overcome internalized negative feelings.

Building a safe, trusting environment is one of the most powerful intervention strategies you can use to help children thrive. If they exhibit evidence of low self-esteem and lack confidence, you must first build or rebuild their sense of trust. Only then can you help them develop their feelings of autonomy. Review the trust-building sequence, then help them feel that they are good, good enough, or worthy. A sense of trust is core to the formation of children's future relationships and social-emotional development. Building or restoring trust is not a single-stage accomplishment. (I discuss building secure relationships and attachments in detail in chapter 3.)

Acknowledge toddlers' and twos' efforts to be autonomous with positive words of encouragement: "You can do it!" or "Look what you can do!" These delight young children and help them develop a positive sense of self. Your encouraging words acknowledge their efforts to become independent. Here's how to help toddlers and twos become autonomous:

- Allow children time to try things by themselves.

- Set limits that still allow children to play and explore.

- Reassure children when you need to set limits.

- Offer children safe choices for playing and exploring.

- Comfort children who become frustrated when they can't master a task.

- Respond to children's need for help when they're trying new activities.

- Verbally acknowledge children's efforts by saying "You can do it!" or "Look what you can do!"

- Talk to children about their new skills and accomplishments.

By the time children reach their third birthdays, their newfound trust and autonomy help them move on successfully to Erikson's other stages of development.

It's Jean Piaget, however, whom I find more useful for thinking about what becomes most vivid at the next stage: young children's cognitive development.

COGNITIVE DEVELOPMENT THEORY

Jean Piaget's (1896–1980) theory of cognitive development proposes that children actively engage in their own learning. This differs from the behaviorism popular in the 1950s and 1960s, when his work first became widely known in this country (Berk 2008). Piaget offered early childhood educators something new about how children learn. He believed that children make sense of the world by constructing their own learning. They are "little scientists," testing out their theories on how objects work and connecting new learning with what they already know or believe. Piaget observed his own children at play and saw how they learned through play. From his observations, he concluded that children take in new experiences and construct or accommodate these to their existing knowledge. They explore the world, test theories, and make sense of the world through these interactions. Their cognition develops, becoming more advanced and sophisticated as they test their theories through trial and error and repetition. They learn to predict what comes next.

Piaget saw children acquiring and building knowledge by accommodating and assimilating the new and the old. As they experiment and experience new information, they try to find places or cognitive structures where their new thoughts or observations will fit. He calls this process *accommodation*. Say, for example, that a child's family has a small brown dog. Initially, the child thinks that all dogs are small and brown, but as he accumulates more experiences of dogs, he begins to realize that not all dogs look like his dog. With the help of responsive adults, he builds his vocabulary and thinking, acquiring a new and much-expanded definition of *dog*.

Piaget called the result of this process *assimilation*: now, the child realizes that dogs come in many sizes and colors. The child's ability to accommodate and assimilate increases as he experiences more interactions with the world. His increasingly sophisticated cognition coincides with his exploding vocabulary and language skills. Cognition and language development go hand-in-hand in his ability to grow and make sense of the world.

According to Piaget, cognitive development has four stages, the first two are most relevant for your work with infants, toddlers, and twos:

Piaget's (1973) Four Stages of Cognitive Development

STAGE	AGE	COGNITIVE TASKS
Sensorimotor	Birth to age two	Infants learn about the world with their eyes, ears, hands, and mouths. Infants use sensorimotor skills to begin solving problems. They develop object permanence and are beginning to understand the properties of objects around them.
Preoperational	Age two to age seven	Children use symbols, such as numbers and words, to represent earlier sensorimotor discoveries. The development of language allows children to engage in pretend play with others. Their developing language and thinking prompts them to ask "Why?" as they learn and make sense of the world.
Concrete operational	Age seven to age eleven	Children's reasoning becomes more logical but is still based in concrete experiences. They are focused on the here and now. Children understand that actions can be reversed.
Formal operational	Age eleven and up	Adolescents have the capacity to think about abstract concepts and other people's ideas. This allows them to think systematically, form hypotheses, and reason deductively about possible real-world situations. This type of thinking is important for long-term planning and consideration of possible outcomes and consequences of actions.

Sensorimotor Stage

During the sensorimotor stage (birth to approximately age two), infants explore the world through sensory and motor experiences. They know the world by tasting, feeling, and touching. When you give them new objects, like books, the first thing they do is put them in their mouths. They spend a lot of time exploring objects orally! While this clearly brings them great pleasure, your response must be to provide safe, nontoxic sensory objects for them to experience. Sensory objects should be tactile and strikingly different (soft, smooth, hard, rough, bumpy, and sticky), so infants can begin constructing knowledge about them.

Providing children with materials to explore ensures that they can have repeated and varied experiences that lead them to deeper and more complex thinking. Take the case of bubbles as an example of how children learn through repeated experiences:

- **Young infants** A young infant watches and observes the colors of bubbles. You explain that bubbles float, and you encourage the child to feel the bubbles' wetness.

- **Older infants** As the child gets older, you revise the activity so she can dip the wand into the soapy water. You model how to blow into the wand, and then you invite the child to try blowing. You say, "Look at the bubbles we're blowing! See all the colors? The colors are red, blue, yellow, and orange. Can you see the colors on the bubbles?" You talk about the way bubbles move in the wind, their different sizes, and how they pop. You might say, "Oh, they pop and disappear! Where do you think they go?"

- **Young toddlers** A young toddler has the skills to move and swing the wand by himself. You describe the activity and help him build vocabulary and concepts like *big* and *little*, *high* and *low*, *floating*, *wet*, *round*, and *shiny*. You encourage him to make bubbles on his own.

- **Older toddlers/twos** The older toddler no longer needs much assistance from you. You can actually step back and document her experiences in your anecdotal record. Invite the child to draw a picture of the bubble activity, and use it to help her recall the experience. Continue to help her build her vocabulary and use of language.

Young children construct knowledge continuously during the sensorimotor stage. By the time they're two, they're starting to understand the properties of objects. By playing with a ball, they discover that the ball rolls and bounces, that it can be soft or bumpy. They use trial and error to gain better understanding of the world. You have probably seen a child putting a small cube inside a box and then taking it out again. What is the child doing—what is the attraction of this

activity? As she repeats this activity, she's learning the properties of cube and box. At the same time, she's developing symbols she can use to represent events and objects.

Preoperational Stage

When children reach two, they enter what Piaget termed the *preoperational stage*, which lasts until about age seven. In this stage, children use symbols, including words, features, pictures, and models, to represent objects and events (Dodge, Rudick, and Berke 2006). They begin to master reasoning and develop magical beliefs. Their interest in why things happen grows. You see this stage in two- and three-year-olds who constantly ask, "Why?"

You can support this sense of wonder by offering them simple answers and helping them learn how things work. Knowing that this period of questioning is a normal stage of cognitive development may help you respond more positively to those seemingly endless "Why?" questions.

During this stage, children also begin to engage in pretend play. With the growing ability to manipulate their environment and their expanding vocabularies, young children can now use objects and mental representations to expand and test their learning. (I discuss mental representation further in chapter 8.) Older toddlers begin to interact and play with peers more cooperatively. In dramatic play, they experiment with objects symbolically. For example, a two-year-old may use a toy phone and mimic a conversation with his mother. Symbolically, he pretends she is on the other end. To do this, he must be able to sustain a mental representation or image of his mother while pretending to talk with her on the phone. When children use mental representations during symbolic play, they are developing their abstract thinking skills. Symbolic play and mental representation set the foundation for abstract reasoning and more advanced cognitive skills. Understanding letters, numbers, abstract thought, and logic is grounded in the sensorimotor and preoperational stages of cognitive development. (I discuss cognitive development further in chapter 8.)

SOCIOCULTURAL THEORY

Lev Vygotsky (1896–1943) developed sociocultural theory, which focuses on how the environment influences children's development. Vygotsky believed that adults, including immediate and extended family and community members, transmit cultural information to the next generation (Berk 2008). He argued that children's culture deeply influences their beliefs, skills, and customs (Kail 2007). For example, children who grow up in families that value reading and knowledge are given books. Reading becomes part of their parent-child interactions. Parents read to their children daily, help them learn to read, and share their belief that reading and learning are important. Vygotsky believed that the way in which information is taught is as important as its content and that adult-child engagement is essential to children's learning.

Zone of Proximal Development

Vygotsky's sociocultural theory assumes that children learn from adults and more experienced peers within their social and cultural network. Vygotsky called the period in which children have not yet fully mastered a task but can perform it with help from a member of their culture the *zone of proximal development*. This theory has led to what researchers and practitioners of ECE now call *scaffolding*.

Scaffolding is an application of sociocultural theory; it describes an adult caregiver's gradual withdrawal of assistance as children construct their own learning. Scaffolding takes many forms: it can involve verbal dialogue or hands-on interactions. For example, you might explain to a child how a jack-in-the-box works. Verbal scaffolding might go like this: you describe how to turn the crank on the box and then ask, "What do you think will happen when you turn the handle?" Physical scaffolding might involve helping the child turn the handle and then encouraging her to do it on her own.

Vygotsky's sociocultural theory can help you effectively scaffold classroom activities. Knowing how children's cognition develops by stages helps you design explanations, prompts, modeling, scaffolding, and thoughtful planning. For example, you might introduce a child to stringing beads, which requires the use of fine-motor skills. You would model how to string a bead and then guide the child while he learns this new skill.

Vygotsky's sociocultural theory is also valuable because of its emphasis on the importance of home culture to children's development. To show your respect for it, you include activities and materials representative of the home environment, like music, songs, and musical instruments. (I discuss partnering with families to strengthen the home-school connection in the closing thoughts at the end of the book.)

ECOLOGICAL SYSTEMS THEORY

American psychologist Urie Bronfenbrenner (1917–2005) viewed child development as an ecological system: children develop through relationships across multiple settings and time. His model consists of four levels: microsystem, mesosystem, exosystem, and macrosystem. Each level is related to and evolves from the previous one and moves toward greater complexity. In the microsystem, children interact daily with the people closest to them, such as parents, siblings, teachers, and peers (Patterson 2009). In the mesosystem, children's relationships extend outward to their school communities and neighbors. The exosystem includes an even wider community: neighborhood, extended family, and parents' work environments. The macrosystem encompasses everything that children encounter, including values, beliefs, customs, culture, and laws.

Young children are often placed in the care of others (such as in child care and educational settings) at the microsystem level, and through interactions there with adults other than family members, they learn about who they are. Although they are influenced primarily by the microsystem, the higher ecological systems also play important parts in young children's development. For example, if a child's mother loses her job because of an economic downturn, the child is directly and indirectly influenced. The loss of family income affects the money available for child care and rent or mortgage; the family may need to move and take the child out of care. If the mother needs to look for work in another community or move closer to a new job, the child may need to leave her familiar program.

As you can see, the child is influenced by many environmental factors; any change in the environment sends ripples into the child-and-family system. Bronfenbrenner proposed that children's development cannot be fully understood unless the environments through which they move are also factored in (Feldman 2007). You can apply Bronfenbrenner's ecological systems theory by working in partnership with families to develop a deeper understanding of their cultures and circumstances.

OTHER CONTEMPORARY THEORIES

The work of T. Berry Brazelton (1918–) and Stanley Greenspan (1941–2010) provide additional recent insight into children's development. Both theorists are physicians who stress the importance of caring early childhood professionals and the value of strong, healthy relationships between teachers, parents, and children. Brazelton's Touchpoints approach addresses key elements found in high-quality ECE and care centers: caregivers with education and training specific to child development; continuity of care for children; and nurturing, positive teacher-child relationships (Brazelton Touchpoints Center 2007). The Touchpoints approach recommends that you build mutually supportive partnerships with parents to increase your understanding of the child and to strengthen the relationship between parents and the child (Singer 2007). Let me give you an example. A parent tells you that she is worried because her twelve-month-old son isn't walking yet. You reassure her that her child is meeting the developmental milestones for physical development. You also remind her that children begin walking at different ages. The mother is relieved. Your response helps the mother learn more about her child's development, which may strengthen the parent-child relationship. She recognizes your knowledge and expertise, which may strengthen your collaborative bond with her. Through such interactions and partnerships, you and the parents build respect and learn more about each other.

Stanley Greenspan is best known for his Developmental, Individual-Difference, Relationship-Based (DIR) therapy and his floortime model. Greenspan worked with emotionally disturbed children and children with autism. He believed that treatment must include assessments of children's emotional and intellectual development and biological challenges that could affect their social interactions (Mercer 2010). His floortime model of assessment and relationship building stresses the importance of adults getting down on the floor with children, supporting their thinking, and engaging in relationship building. He believed that teachers and children should spend plenty of time together on the floor, building the children's capacity to engage with adults warmly and pleasurably. He thought that adults could communicate with gestures and words more easily on the floor with the children. Greenspan's relationship-based theory provides support for you in its emphasis on the importance of responsive caregiving and relationship building among parents, teachers, and children.

FINAL THOUGHTS

Early childhood theories contribute to our collective knowledge of how children grow and develop. Erik Erikson's psychosocial theory describes human development in terms of lifetime stages. Erikson identified the main tasks of infants and toddlers as forming trusting relationships with their primary caregivers and developing au-

tonomy. Jean Piaget provided new insights into how children think and construct learning. Vygotsky and Bronfenbrenner emphasized the importance of culture and environment in children's development. Researchers T. Berry Brazelton and Stanley Greenspan extended the study of children with new approaches and through observation and assessment. They recognized the importance of teacher-training, relationship building, and providing nurturing care environments for young children.

You can use these developmental theories to better understand early attachment and the four learning domains. I'll explain how to apply each of these areas of early development to best practices in infant-toddler caregiving in the following chapters.

WHAT CAREGIVERS CAN DO

- Respond to the needs of infants by holding and rocking them gently.
- Calm and soothe crying children.
- Introduce new toys and materials to your classroom.
- Recognize children's efforts to try new activities.
- Use positive language, such as "Look what you can do!"
- Create situations in which you can scaffold children's learning.
- Ask parents to share music and materials from their home cultures.
- Respond to parents' concerns positively and respectfully.
- Build collaborative partnerships with parents.

BIG IDEAS FOR CAREGIVERS

- Responsive caregivers react to infants' needs in nurturing, caring ways.
- Propelled by their natural curiosity, children construct learning by experimenting with the world around them.
- Mutual interactions between adults and children are essential to children's learning.

REFLECTION AND APPLICATION

1. List three reasons why it's important for children to feel safe and nurtured in your early care environment.
2. How do children construct their own learning, and how can you support their efforts?
3. How can you apply your understanding of theories of development to your interactions with young children?
4. How can you apply your understanding of the trust-building sequence to your work with infants and toddlers?

Building Secure Relationships and Attachments

Building secure relationships and attachments are primary tasks for children's first three years of life. The relationships people form throughout life are shaped by their earliest ones. When these are loving and nurturing, children learn how to love, care, and form close, intimate relationships with others. In secure relationships, individuals trust and feel safe, respected, and valued. Children can and should be in secure relationships with many people. In high-quality early care environments, children form secure relationships with their caregivers. When you are sensitive to infants' and toddlers' physical and emotional needs, providing them with predictable environments

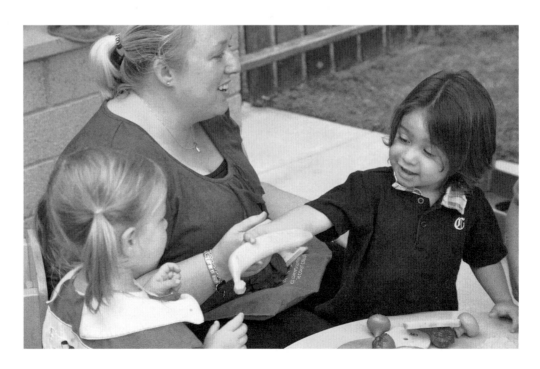

and continuity of care, children learn to form secure relationships. These don't need to be long lasting in order to provide them with a deep sense of security, but the relationships must be positive, caring, and responsive.

Like secure relationships, secure attachments allow children to feel protected, comforted, and loved. Attachments are more complex than the relationships that anchor and initiate them. They develop between an infant and one or two specific, stable adults, typically parents or another primary adult in the child's life. Such attachments are deeper and more profound than other relationships. Because secure attachments are so important to children's development, those of you who care for infants and toddlers must understand how these attachments are formed and what roles they play in every early relationship that young children form.

In high-quality early care programs, infants and toddlers form secure relationships with their primary caregivers. Primary care is considered a best practice because it helps young children establish these healthy relationships. You can help children form secure attachments with their parents and other primary adults in their lives. Part of the way you do this is by encouraging parents to remain connected to their children while they attend child care. Communicating with parents daily is essential to quality care. You should inform parents about their children's daily activities and progress across the developmental domains. Show respect and sensitivity to parents' relationships with their children, and offer them opportunities to volunteer in your room. (Chapter 5 offers you advice on designing the ECE environment to support attachment between parents and children; I discuss your partnership with parents further in the closing thoughts at the end of the book.)

Research demonstrates a strong correlation between children's secure attachment, emotional well-being, and mental health. (I discuss evidence that attachment is linked to healthy social-emotional development in chapter 6.)

THEORIES OF ATTACHMENT

Theories of attachment were first proposed in the work of Harry Harlow (1905–81) in the 1950s. Harlow's research still influences how early childhood professionals view mother-infant relationships. In his famous study, Harlow put young rhesus monkeys in a cage with two wire surrogate mothers. One provided only food. The other provided no nourishment but was covered in a soft towel. Although the infant monkeys sought food from the wire mother, when they were left alone, they cuddled up only to the softly wrapped mother (Harlow 1958). Their behavior demonstrated that warmth and comfort were as necessary as food for optimal survival. Harlow's research caught the attention of psychiatrist John Bowlby (1907–90), who extended Harlow's work on attachment and examined how to apply it to human behavior.

Bowlby proposed that parent-infant interactions produce emotional ties, which he termed *attachment*. He believed that the quality of an infant's attachment to the parent forms the basis for the child's feeling of security and his capacity to form trusting relationships throughout life (Berk 2008). He speculated that the infant's ability to cry constitutes an innate ability to signal parents and other caregivers, the first step in connecting to others and forming attachments to them. Emotional connections between parents and infants create secure attachments.

Bowlby's emphasis on the importance of parent-child relationships influences early childhood professionals' work with parents and children today. It has led to the now-widespread belief that proximity to caring adults is critical to children's development (Patterson 2009). Bowlby addressed the negative effects of unresponsive and ambivalent caregiving on children's emotional well-being and mental health. Like Erikson, he viewed trust as a central component in children's ability to form enduring, loving, and intimate relationships.

Expanding on Bowlby's work, Mary Ainsworth (1913–99) studied infants' responses to separation. Her research demonstrated how infants' behavior changes when they are exposed to strangers and separated from the adults with whom they have formed secure attachments. Ainsworth observed that infants vary in their degree of security when separated from their parents. Her research identified three types of attachment:

- secure attachment

- avoidant attachment

- resistant/ambivalent attachment

A fourth type of attachment, called *disorganized attachment*, was identified in 1986 by Mary Main and Judith Solomon.

Secure Attachment

Ainsworth noticed that some infants are content and confident in the presence of their parents. Securely attached children sense that they are safe and provided for in the presence of the attached person, usually a parent. Such children seek the company of their parents only when they need security, protection, and comfort. Ainsworth termed these children *securely attached* to the stable adults in their lives. She theorized that secure attachments between parents and children are the cornerstone of emotional well-being for young children and the foundation of their future relationships. Children who form secure attachments during their first three years are likely to develop close, loving, and lasting relationships as adults.

Avoidant Attachment

Children who do not seek out a parent for comfort or security and who do not believe that the attachment figure or adult will protect or provide for them, who do not cry or seem upset when the adult is absent, and who instead avoid proximity to the adult exhibit what Ainsworth termed *avoidant attachment*. The adults in these children's lives do not provide safety, protection, or comfort. As children with avoidant attachment grow older, they may hide or suppress their feelings by not forming close relationships with others.

Resistant/Ambivalent Attachment

Children who experience ambivalence or uncertainly in response to their attachment figures form what Ainsworth termed *resistant/ambivalent attachments*. Such children are unsure if an adult will protect or provide for them. As a result, they exhibit a mixture of approach and avoidance in the adult's presence. They may be anxious and clingy with other adults— for example, with you—but remain distant from their primary adult figure. Children with ambivalent attachment may be difficult to comfort and may resist physical contact. Their inability to trust the world and the adults in it may lead to problems with forming lasting, close, and intimate relationships later in life.

Disorganized Attachment

As its name implies, this is the most unpredictable and inconsistent form of attachment. It's also the most rare. Children with disorganized attachment do not shape their behaviors around the attachment figure. Their behaviors can appear bizarre and random; their actions and reactions to the attachment figure are incongruent. They may allow the adult to pick them up but then stiffen at the adult's touch. They may cry, freeze, or stare blankly into the distance. They may make poor eye contact and appear distant and unresponsive to the adult. Children exposed to traumatic events, including severe abuse, neglect, and isolation, are most at risk for developing disorganized attachment. They find forming close, loving relationships with others challenging. As adults, they typically have difficulty forming lasting, intimate relationships. Their early exposure to trauma may predispose them to anxiety and depression.

Children who form secure attachments and relationships with caring adults show signs of trust and autonomy across Erikson's early stages of development. As they

grow older, they develop positive behaviors, including initiative and industry, the next stage in Erikson's model. The first three years of life help children develop feelings of security, confidence, and sense of self; these are the foundation for the other skills they need for their social-emotional development. (I discuss this further in chapter 6.)

I mentioned in chapter 2 that T. Berry Brazelton encourages relationships between caregivers, parents, and children. He recognizes that children can form secure relationships with caregivers while maintaining secure attachments to their parents. He assures parents that babies may adore their caregivers and still love their parents more (Brazelton, accessed 2012). He knows that parents need the support of knowledgeable caregivers when they start parenting, and that competent, caring professionals need training, knowledge, and expertise to help new parents. He is convinced that parents and caregivers must support each other when they're providing care for young children.

You should recognize the signs of secure attachments between children and adults. Babies with secure attachments demonstrate a number of behaviors:

- They show delight when they see their parents.

- They relax and gaze into your eyes while feeding.

- They sit close to and cuddle up with familiar adults.

- They come to familiar adults and raise their arms to be picked up.

- They come to familiar adults when they fall or get hurt.

- They coo, babble, and try to communicate.

- They smile and move their bodies to connect with familiar adults.

- They engage in play with familiar adults.

- They laugh and show joyful enthusiasm.

In high-quality early learning environments, responsive caregivers help parents form secure attachments with their children. Here are some ways you can help parents:

- Communicate with parents daily about their children's activities, including eating, sleeping, toileting, and playing.

- Offer parents a quiet place to say good-bye to their children every day.

- Provide nursing mothers with a quiet, peaceful place to breast-feed.

- Post daily routines, schedules, and special activities for parents to see.

- Encourage parents to drop by and see their children during the day.

- Respect cultural beliefs and family values; integrate these into the children's care.

To help parents feel connected while their children are in your care, encourage them to ask about their babies' daily activities and developmental progress. Learning about the stages of growth and development helps parents understand their children's journey and progress. Share information and resources with new parents, and offer them materials that can ease their fears about being new parents. Encourage them to talk about any changes at home that might influence their children's usual activities, such as eating or sleeping, and any concerns they have as their children form relationships with others. (I discuss partnerships with parents further in the closing thoughts at the end of the book.)

FINAL THOUGHTS

Over the past sixty years, researchers have linked the emotional well-being of children to the formation of their earliest attachments and relationships. Healthy, secure relationships and attachments arise from the bonds that babies form with warm, nurturing, stable adults. These persist throughout life. Although children can form more than one secure attachment, parents are typically the primary source of security for most young children. Early attachment researcher Harry Harlow demonstrated that young primates need physical comfort and closeness as well as food. John Bowlby theorized that infants' innate ability to cry means that they can start to connect and form attachment at birth, while Mary Ainsworth and her colleagues expanded

Bowlby's work by identifying three types of attachment. T. Berry Brazelton furthered our understanding of relationships and attachment by stressing the importance of strong relationships between caregivers and parents.

Whether you look at the work of these researchers or the evidence of your own observations, and I hope you do both, you can't emphasize the importance of early attachments and relationships too much. They are the foundation of trust and security throughout life.

WHAT CAREGIVERS CAN DO

- Talk to parents about their children's growth and development.
- Encourage your program to adopt continuity of care as a policy.
- Respond to the needs of individual children in loving, nurturing ways.
- Follow daily routines and class schedules so children have a stable, predictable environment.
- Give parents information on the developmental stages of infancy and toddlerhood.
- Create a setting in which children and parents feel supported.
- Partner with families to care for their children.

BIG IDEAS FOR CAREGIVERS

- Early relationships shape future relationships.
- Secure attachments begin in infancy and endure throughout life.
- Children can form secure relationships with more than one caregiver and still maintain secure attachments to their parents.

REFLECTION AND APPLICATION

1. How can you support secure attachments between children and their primary attachment figures?
2. What can you do to better support parent-child relationships?
3. How do you build secure relationships with the children in your care?
4. What can you do to make your relationships with children even more secure?
5. What three things can you do to build a trusting, safe environment?
6. Create a plan to strengthen secure relationships for a child who has just started in your program.

Influences on Early Learning

What we know about child development keeps evolving. Brain imaging now gives us clearer pictures of how children's brains develop, while behavioral research helps us better understand temperament, developmentally appropriate practices (DAP), and the importance of play. When you're thinking about building relationships with young children and designing high-quality learning environments for them, you should incorporate this new knowledge into your program. A good starting point is pondering the roles played by nature and nurture in young children's lives.

Every child is born with a specific genetic makeup that determines traits including eye and hair color, eventual height, and predisposition for certain skills. We call these components *nature*. And every child is born into a culture that interprets and understands experiences differently. Families and other people who care for young children influence children's development by the experiences they do (and don't) expose children to. We call these components *nurture*.

Your challenge, like that of their families, is to offer children experiences and places that are rich in language and activities instead of deprived and scanty. The debate over nature versus nurture has raged since at least the seventeenth century, and it's unlikely to be resolved anytime soon, but most early childhood professionals do agree that high-quality settings and highly qualified caregivers are critical to young children's emotional well-being and development. You can influence children's development positively by offering them experiences that stimulate their brains and maximize their ability to think and learn.

BRAIN DEVELOPMENT

Human brains start to develop four weeks after conception, when the neural tube—the beginning of the central nervous system—begins to form. The neural tube produces nerve cells, called *neurons*, through rapid cell division. By the time children are born, their brains consist of billions of neurons. That's *nature* speaking. During the first few years of life, the connections among these nerve cells can be either strengthened or weakened by children's experiences—and that's *nurture* speaking. The strengthening or weakening of neuronal connections shapes children's brains for life.

Why? Because neurons store and process information. At one end of each neuron, dendrites receive information from adjoining cells and pass it through the cell to the axons—long, strandlike fibers at the other end of each neuron. In turn, axons pass along information to the dendrites of nearby neurons. Think of it as a relay system. None of these connectors, nor the cell bodies themselves, touches another; there's a gap between them. That gap is called the *synapse*. Synaptic connections are necessary to the survival of all living things as well as to development across the learning domains.

The dendrites of one neuron connect with the axons of another cell by chemical transmission across the synapse. These chemical transmitters are called *neural transmitters*. Glial cells support neurons by providing a myelin sheath that coats the axon and increases the speed by which information is processed across the axon. This process of encasing axons is called *myelination*. The myelination process begins before birth and continues into adolescence. If neurons are not stimulated by neural transmitters across the synaptic gap, they do not survive; their death is called *synaptic pruning*. It is critical that young children's brains be stimulated so that they can make as many connections as possible.

The child's brain is more flexible during the first three years of life than at any other time. Researchers call the young brain's susceptibility to pruning and stimulation *plasticity*: the brain can change and adapt with almost terrifying ease. Because young brains are so profoundly affected by the presence—or absence—of experiences, you should capitalize on their plasticity by offering children enriched, stimulating environments. When you respond warmly and caringly to babies' cries, their brains make positive connections. In other words, by providing a wide variety of rich experiences, you ensure the optimal growth of young, developing brains. (My companion book, *Activities for Responsive Caregiving: Infants, Toddlers, and Twos,* offers a variety of activities to stimulate cognitive development.)

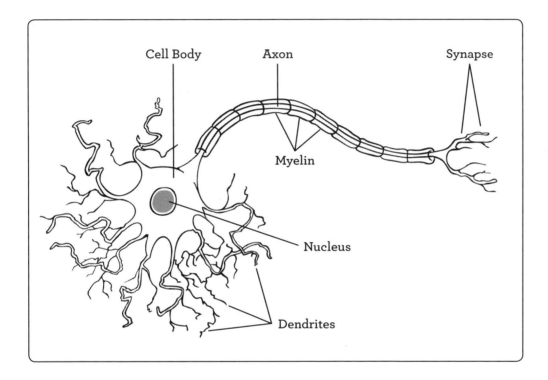

But that's not all! Different areas of the brain are primarily responsible for different functions. The brain has two hemispheres connected by a network of nerve fibers. The left hemisphere guides language and sequential thinking, while the right one guides emotions and spatial relationships like pattern recognition, drawing, and music. Talking, reading, and singing to children stimulates different parts of their developing brains, strengthens synaptic connections, and prunes synapses. It's also important that children cross their midline while engaging in everyday activities—taking the left hand to the right side of the body and the right hand across to the left side of the body. The richest environments and experiences stimulate both hemispheres of children's brains so they can develop simultaneously.

Such early intervention is even more important for children who have developmental delays. If you notice signs of such delays in children you care for, discuss them as soon as possible with the child's parents and help them locate practitioners who can provide developmental screenings.

TEMPERAMENT

Each child is born with a unique temperament; here we encounter the *nature* component again, for temperament is considered innate and stable over time (Churchill 2003). Temperament influences how children interact with peers and adults, and how they respond to routines, frustration, and discomfort. Temperaments affect how children assimilate information, react to noises, accommodate stimuli, adapt to change, and warm to other people. As a responsive caregiver, you should be sensitive to the temperaments of the infants, toddlers, and twos in your care and adapt your style of caregiving to each of them.

Temperament is particularly important to consider in thinking about how children form relationships and interact with others. One well-known study of temperament types was conducted by Alexander Thomas, Stella Chess, and Herbert G. Birch (1970), who studied a group of children from infancy through adulthood. Their longitudinal study provides the framework for a system that classifies infant temperament into three categories:

Temperament

TYPE	CHARACTERISTICS
Easy	Easy infants are usually happy, establish routines easily, and adapt quickly to changed circumstances. Their feeding and sleeping habits are regular, and when they become toddlers, they easily learn to use the toilet. They are cheerful and respond to distress with only mild frustration. Their temperament makes them easy to care for; they adapt well to early care settings.
Difficult	Difficult infants display intensely negative reactions, adjust with difficulty to family routines, and resist change. Napping and sleeping through the night are difficult for them. They cry loudly, fuss more, and adapt to change slowly. They are often moody and have violent tantrums. Caregivers who don't understand this temperament type may find caring for these children difficult. It's best to match difficult children with caregivers who can offer them optimal patience and understanding.
Slow-to-warm-up	Slow-to-warm infants are relatively inactive and adjust slowly to new situations and change. Their moods are often negative, though this may not be apparent in group settings. They warm to new situations slowly and may cling to adults when pressured to join a group before they are ready. Caregivers should pay special attention to how they introduce and pace new activities for slow-to-warm children. Offer them opportunities at a pace slow enough to complement their temperament.

Providing optimal care to young children, whatever their temperament, is one of your responsibilities. You must understand children's temperaments and be sensitive to how they respond to different situations if you are to successfully group and find suitable caregivers for them. What's termed *goodness of fit* between children and adults has a demonstrably positive effect on children's cognitive and social development (Churchill 2003). *Goodness of fit* refers to how children and caregivers relate to each other and "the nature and demands of the environment" (Feldman 2007, 195). You might want to pair children who are fussy or slow-to-warm with caregivers who are warm, gentle, and willing to introduce children slowly to new experiences and to encourage their efforts.

If you're finding it hard to respond positively to or you're becoming impatient with some children, you should carefully evaluate the situation before moving them to someone else's care. Programs need to provide physically and emotionally safe environments for *all* children and do what's best for them. Quick fixes are seldom the solution. Thoughtful discussions between staff, parents, and the director should precede any move. All children need your patience and consideration. No matter how aggravating their behaviors, difficult children give you the chance to teach them how to communicate more effectively, learn self-control, and get along with others. Try to use those occasions when children challenge you to learn more about their temperaments, improve your own interpersonal skills, and expand your knowledge of child development.

Knowing more about temperament helps you to plan and to interpret children's behavior so you can support their development better. For example, difficult and slow-to-warm children may need to have activities introduced differently than children with easier temperaments. (You can read more about temperament characteristics in children birth to age three on the website of the National Association for the Education of Young Children [NAEYC], www.naeyc.org, and the website of Zero to Three, www.zerotothree.org.)

TODDLER TEMPERAMENT

Toddlerhood is a time of rapidly changing feelings and moods. Toddlers may exhibit difficult, challenging temperament-driven behaviors like tantrums or prolonged crying. They may hit or bite one minute and then gently comfort a peer the next. They are often frustrated while acquiring new skills like learning to share. It's not uncommon even for children with easygoing temperaments to flare up occasionally. But temperament is stable and consistent, so most children's episodes of tantrums and crying are short and become more so as they grow older and learn new skills. Once toddlers become more skillful at communicating their needs and managing their feelings, they exhibit fewer challenging behaviors.

LEARNING ENVIRONMENTS

Learning environments should convey respect for children's temperaments and stages of development. High-quality programs provide DAP for infants, toddlers,

and two-year-olds. DAP has become a common term used in the field of early childhood education to encompass a range of caregiving and teaching practices designed to support children's ages, developmental stages, and special needs. It also addresses the program's physical environment: the furniture, lighting, napping areas, changing rooms, eating areas, play materials, manipulatives, and art supplies.

Developmentally appropriate learning environments and practices give children optimal time and space in which to learn new skills and build on existing competencies. In developmentally appropriate early care, children's needs are dealt with quickly. Children are talked with and listened to respectfully. Caregivers understand the importance of nurturing the whole child and offering opportunities to grow and develop across the learning domains. In healthy programs, caregivers and families support each other and talk openly about how to engage children at home and in the program.

THE IMPORTANCE OF PLAY

Children learn and grow through play; play is the business of childhood. Young children engage in play fully, using their bodies and their brains. Playing integrates their emotions, teaches them to solve problems, and to learn language; it develops their imaginations. Play isn't something children automatically do—they need to learn how to play through playful engagement, first from adults and later from their peers. You can model and scaffold play for them. When you sing, tickle, and kiss babies and toddlers, you stimulate their brains and build relationships with them. Help toddlers enjoy their new physical skills by encouraging them to push and pull toys, climb up and down slides, and ride tricycles. They develop their skills by sharing and playing with peers in the sandbox or the dramatic play area. Play teaches them how to interact with others in a fun way.

Play starts when infants and caregivers build relationships. Babies imitate your gestures and expressions and develop confidence

in their ability to manipulate the world. When you watch infants and toddlers, you can see that they're busy learning through sensory exploration, manipulation, and trial and error. Infants spend most of their playtime alone or with a responsive caregiver. As they grow, they become more aware of other people and pay closer attention to their peers in the parallel play common among toddlers. As their language, cognitive, and motor skills increase, they begin to play cooperatively. By the time they reach their third birthdays, most children are using their developing imaginations and social skills to pretend play with others.

Respond to children's growing skills by planning play-based activities. Make those activities ones that allow children to direct and lead their own play. Arrange settings and materials so that children can play freely and safely. This doesn't mean that you can be disengaged—on the contrary, you should be scaffolding children's play. Watch and observe them, and provide support and guidance that's developmentally appropriate. Ask open-ended questions to hold children's attention, show approval of their play, and work to increase their sense of self and self-esteem. Introduce new learning materials so children can acquire new skills and reach their developmental milestones. Remember that child-directed activities strengthen your relationship with them, too, as well as enhance children's conviction that learning is fun.

Keep in mind that children differ in their tolerance for length and intensity of play activities. One child might enjoy long periods of rough-and-tumble play, while another might whimper and cry at such intense activity. This second child might prefer a short period of quiet, relaxed play, such as sorting cubes or stringing beads.

Develop your understanding of the cues that babies and toddlers provide when they're feeling under- or overstimulated. Babies who are understimulated might cry or smile at you in order to engage you in play. They might also move their arms and legs to get your attention. Understimulated toddlers might bring you a toy or a book to signal that they want to be read to or played with. Overstimulated babies often cry and look away from their caregivers. Overstimulated toddlers might run from one activity to another, unable to decide what to do next. They might also cry or have a tantrum. Show your respect for infants and toddlers by reading their cues accurately and adapting the environment to their needs. Here's what you can do to support children's play activities:

- Respond to the cues children offer about their preferred length and intensity of play activities.

- Model how to play, using animated expressions.

- Talk to the children while you play, using silly voices.

- Imitate children's use of a toy and then model an expanded use of that toy.

- Provide children with the time and space to play alone and with peers.

- Join children on the floor while engaging in playful activities.

- Provide toys that offer different levels of difficulty across the learning domains (for example, puzzles and toys that elicit counting, sorting, and categorizing).

- Introduce new toys one at a time, so children can explore and play with each of them.

Every adult has a personal, playful style, and infants quickly learn to identify those of their parents and caregivers. You can help parents understand and enjoy their roles as their children's first teachers and to value play as the engine of their children's learning.

Helping parents play with their children supports healthy relationships and developmental competencies. When home and early care settings are equally playful, children receive the consistent message that learning is fun. They also learn that they remain themselves in these different settings. Differentiating self and others is an important step for children in developing their sense of self and self-identity.

Infants play primarily with adults. As they get older, they start to watch other children play. Older infants and young toddlers start with solitary play and move on to parallel and then cooperative play. They develop their social-emotional skills by playing with peers: they learn to share, take turns, manage emotions, and acquire patience. Play increases their receptive and expressive language and brings the world to them through their motor and perceptual skills. Offer children a variety of activities and educational toys to explore freely. Developmentally appropriate environments always make play central to learning.

FINAL THOUGHTS

When you care for infants and toddlers, consider the enormous influences of nature and nurture on them. Technologies like magnetic resonance imaging (MRI) have provided new insights into the growing brains of infants and toddlers. We now know that environments that stimulate neural connections help children's brains become more specialized. Early interventions are particularly critical in helping children maximize their learning potential. Understanding temperament types can help you interpret children's responses to routines, frustrations, and discomfort. Once you understand temperaments, you can adapt your caregiving strategies to the individual temperament of each child. Using a variety of play-based, developmentally appropriate practices, you can respond respectfully and effectively to the cultural and linguistic needs of each child in your care.

WHAT CAREGIVERS CAN DO

- Provide a variety of activities, such as reading, singing, and playing music.
- Provide varied sensory experiences.
- Take children on walks outside and explain what you see.
- Talk to children throughout the day.
- Adapt your caregiving responses to the temperament characteristics of each child.
- Be patient with children who show signs of frustration.
- Design your environment to help children reach developmental goals.
- Respond to children's cues that they want to play.
- Plan and engage in play with children.

BIG IDEAS FOR CAREGIVERS

- Developing brains are stimulated by rich activities.
- Children possess unique temperaments.
- Play is the business of childhood.

REFLECTION AND APPLICATION

1. Name three things you can do to support infants' developing brains.
2. Name three things you can do to support toddlers' developing brains.
3. How can you care for children of different temperaments?
4. Name three ways you can increase your play activities with children.
5. Using DAP, create a plan that will improve your teaching strategies and interactions with the children in your care.

Responsive Learning Environments

To deliver quality care, you need to build responsive learning environments. Such environments are reassuring, inclusive, and physically safe spaces. And behind the scenes, they are supported by policies and practices that keep your spaces, and everyone and everything in them, healthy and safe. This chapter discusses these elements and points out how they fit into providing children with the best possible learning opportunities.

DESIGNING THE ENVIRONMENT

You already understand that high-quality environments have a big impact on the growth and development of very young children and that early childhood education (ECE) and care settings should promote children's learning. Many children spend the majority of their days (sometimes their nights) eating, sleeping, and playing in early care settings. Not surprisingly, organizations that advocate for young children make recommendations for how programs should design their settings. These best practices cover health and safety, inclusiveness, and curricula.

Environments should be designed from the ground up, and by that I mean with the health, safety, and needs of children as their founda-

tion. They should be welcoming to all children and their families. Indoor and outdoor areas alike should encourage free movement and children's mastery of new skills. Spaces should be organized into many areas, most of which are accessible to children. Objects for play should be plentiful and well organized.

Anita Olds (2001) has observed that physical space is one of the biggest environmental barriers for children with special needs. For an early care environment to be truly high quality, its spaces—indoors and outdoors—should be barrier free to all children. Children need to be able to move around and interact freely with people and objects in order to learn.

Welcome Space

Families need a pleasant place to say their good-byes each time a child returns to your program. This place should send parents a powerful message that you care about their children. Your welcome space is a good place to display your personal caregiving philosophy statement (see page 5). Every child should have a cubby here. Affix children's first names and photographs to their cubbies; toddlers quickly learn to spot their spaces and start using them for their personal belongings. Put up a family board, and post information about your room's daily schedule, upcoming activities and events, and parenting resources. A whiteboard is a terrific addition to your welcome space because you can easily add and erase reminders to families, along with other short-term information. Post photographs of the children enjoying classroom activities in this area too; these help families understand what their children's days are like and make them feel more connected to their children. Design a quiet space within or adjacent to the welcome space where nursing mothers can breastfeed their babies. Make sure it's separate from the area where families drop off and pick up children, and that it's insulated from classroom noises. The welcome space should look warm and inviting, because this is where children make the transition from home and parents into your classroom.

Indoor Space

Best practices recommend that indoor spaces offer distinctive areas for active exploring and quiet, peaceful activities. Organize indoor spaces so children can be in close contact with you and other caregivers. Infants need to be held and carried, and toddlers and twos need room to explore and play. Make sure that spaces for infant care have soft, low furniture. Low, carpeted risers help mobile infants practice crawling

up and down. Areas for toddlers and twos should be scaled to them and reflect their stages of development. For example, you can install a low mattress so that toddlers who are learning to stand or walk can stabilize themselves. Provide toddlers who can easily stand with a low table and manipulatives like puzzles that they can work with. Make sure there's enough room so every child can sit, roll, crawl, and walk without hurting herself or someone else.

Tummy time helps infants develop the muscles and motor skills they need to reach their next physical milestones and start rolling over, sitting, and standing. Make tummy time something they look forward to! Provide infants with lots of things to look at and objects to play with, like soft balls, cloth books, small mirrors, and sorting cubes. (I discuss physical development further in chapter 7.)

Once children begin moving on their own, they quickly learn the difference between the textures of carpet, tile, and wood. As they roll, crawl, and take their first steps on these different surfaces, they learn to adjust their movements to the different surfaces beneath their feet and bellies. They discover if the floor is slippery, smooth, or rough. They may need to try moving across a new kind of surface several times in order to figure out how to negotiate it. Make sure that carpets are soft, warm, and free of tears or frays and that floors are draft free.

Organize spaces to accommodate the age group that uses it most often. Infant spaces should contain a reading corner with plenty of cloth and hard-covered books, walls with low mirrors, quiet places for napping, and open spaces for crawling and exploring. Toddlers and twos need low tables for manipulatives and sensory activities, large pillows to plop on, places to build with soft blocks, and areas for dramatic play.

Toys and materials should offer a range of difficulty so children can practice mastering skills. Materials that don't fit onto low tables should be placed on low shelves or in baskets or tubs so they're easy for toddlers to reach. Best practices recommend that toy shelves and bookshelves should be labeled with the name and picture of what's available so children can start to make connections between real-world objects and printed words.

I can't say enough good things about using mirrors in early childhood spaces! You already know that infants love looking at themselves in mirrors, but there's much more to mirrors than that. Developmentally, mirrors are valuable because they help children feel more secure by reflecting what's around them. They tell children that they're separate and distinct individuals. Place acrylic safety mirrors—handheld and secure low-wall mirrors—throughout the area so children can see their reflections. Help children learn to differentiate themselves from others by pointing out their facial features to them.

If it's within your power, make sure that children's environments don't include sharp corners and edges. If you must, pad the corners of walls with bumper guards and corner moldings to protect young, unsteady crawlers and walkers. Complement the coziness of your well-organized toys and books with walls that are low-key in color. Earth tones (such as tan and beige) and off-white walls help make rooms feel warm and calming. You might choose bright colors for accents, but avoid painting or papering walls with bright, saturated colors—they can be overstimulating and distracting to young children. Ideally, most of the light in your classroom by day will be natural, but artificial light is needed on overcast days. Make sure artificial light is warm toned and soothing.

Lights, temperature, sounds, and textures provide sensory stimulation to developing children. Get down on the floor and look around from their perspective: see how light reflects off the floors and windows, and adjust lighting so children aren't exposed to glare. Adjust the heating and cooling systems so the air is comfortable near the floor. Muffle the inevitable noise with carpets and rugs.

Plexiglass can be used for room dividers to offer children clear views of other children, adults, and play activities. Plexiglass display centers are perfect for displaying photographs, drawings, and print. If you mount a plexiglass learning center on the wall, you can slip images of people, animals, and objects behind it, changing the display whenever children become interested in a new topic. You can use the display area to talk with children about their explorations, to build their vocabularies, and to foster their classroom relationships. Just be sure the plexiglass sheets don't have ragged or sharp edges.

Let's not forget about children's most fundamental physical needs. Provide safe spaces for diapering, toileting, hand washing, and eating. Food preparation, feeding, and eating areas should be separate from spaces used for other physical needs. Each of these areas should be designed so you can easily see and reach all of the children.

Quiet Spaces

Infants, toddlers, and twos need quiet, peaceful places in which to relax. Creating these spaces can be quite a challenge in a room full of exuberant young children. You'll have to carve out quiet areas away from the noise of busy areas. The most likely location is near sleeping or reading corners. Quiet spaces give young children the chance to learn about and savor privacy. You can provide mattresses or extra-large pillows so the children can plop down and relax. Fish tanks, soft cuddly toys, and a variety of books are fine additions to your quiet spaces.

Sleeping Areas

Babies sleep a lot, so designing spaces that help infants and toddlers sleep well should be one of your priorities. Your state has licensing requirements regarding infant and toddler sleeping areas, including cribs. Follow these, of course, but supplement them with developmentally appropriate practices that encourage restful sleep. Use low lighting, dimmer switches, and soft music to help children sleep. Make sure your sleeping areas are equipped with rockers or gliders to use for soothing crying or fussy babies. Each infant should have a separate crib, and each toddler and two-year-old should have his own cot and bedding.

One sleep safety best practice you'll want to implement is the recommendation that all infants be placed on their backs to sleep. Research on sudden infant death syndrome (SIDS) tells us that more infants have died of SIDS when they sleep on their stomachs than those who sleep on their backs. In 1994, the National Institute of Child Health and Human Development (NICHD 2005) and the American Academy of Pediatrics started recommending that infants be placed on their backs at night and during naps. In response, medical professionals organized the Safe to Sleep campaign, which teaches parents and caregivers the importance of placing babies on their backs to sleep. You should follow these recommendations and emphasize their importance to parents. You can obtain more information and Safe to Sleep brochures to hand out to parents on NICHD's website, www.nichd.nih.gov.

Familiarize yourself with the Safe to Sleep campaign's recommendations—there's more to them than placing babies on their backs. For example, babies should not be allowed to sleep on sofas, waterbeds, or other soft surfaces. Pillows, stuffed animals, and quilts or blankets should not be placed in cribs. Mattresses should be firm. Overheating should be avoided: infants' faces and heads should not be covered while they're sleeping.

Several risk factors for SIDS are now recognized. Children two to four months are most at risk, and babies of African American and American Indian descent are especially vulnerable, as are infants who are born prematurely, had low birth weight, or are born to very young or alcohol- or drug-dependent mothers (NICHD 2005). Be sure to acquaint parents and other caregiving adults with Safe to Sleep's potentially life-saving guidelines.

Outdoor Space

As a responsive caregiver, you understand how important it is for infants, toddlers, and twos to play outdoors. Outdoor play relaxes children, diffuses tension, calms fussy babies, and tires out overly active toddlers. Being outside gives children opportunities to explore and learn about nature. Playing outdoors provides additional opportunities for children to problem-solve and develop cooperative-play skills. Outdoor spaces also help children feel connected to the big, beautiful world and what can be found there: sunlight, fresh air, the feel of wind and sun on their skin.

So how do you organize outdoor spaces to make them inviting, invigorating—*and safe*? Think about them the way you do indoor spaces: each age group needs a space appropriate to its needs. Low benches allow mobile infants and toddlers to climb onto your lap to sing a song or hear a story. Nonmobile infants need shaded blankets so they can look up at the trees and have outdoor tummy time. Swings offer soft places for you to rock and comfort infants— the outdoor equivalent of rockers and gliders.

Toddlers and twos view outdoor spaces very differently than infants, and they want to *go!* So make sure they can move freely outdoors, pushing and pulling their wheeled toys, riding their tricycles, and rooting around in sandboxes. Provide plenty of sturdy books, and chalk for drawing on cement areas. Sensory tables and water activities are not only great fun for young children, they also introduce new textures and teach cause and effect. Children can paint outdoors with greater abandon than indoors; easels are particularly good for outdoor use. Supply your outdoor spaces with balls, cars, bubbles, and water paints. If Duplos and other blocks are

popular in your program, stock your outdoor space with small tables and chairs where children can play with their building materials.

In some programs, outdoor spaces are challengingly large. Make sure you can see all the children at all times. Free outdoor play does not mean that you can ignore adult-to-child ratios; children must be as closely supervised outdoors as in. Depending on your climate and latitude, you may also need to carefully monitor children's exposure to wind and sun.

HEALTH AND SAFETY

High-quality programs honor best practices for adult-to-child ratios and health and safety; the physical health and safety of children are as important as their emotional well-being. That's why every state issues its own health and safety requirements, and licensed programs must adhere to those guidelines. High-quality programs meet or exceed these standards. Here I cover proper hygiene, hand washing, cleaning and sanitizing, nutrition, and mealtime practices. (I discuss other components elsewhere—for example, adult-to-child ratios, which appear in chapter 1.)

Proper Hygiene and Hand Washing

The first line of defense against the spread of pathogens is effective hygiene and hand washing. Emphasize and monitor hand washing among the adults and children in your program—no one step is as effective in preventing the spread of disease. Infants in particular are susceptible to infectious diseases, so preventing the spread of pathogens is important. You must wash hands routinely before and after feeding and diapering children. Assist children in washing their faces and hands, and teach them how to do it properly. You can post photographs or illustrations on hand washing so children see graphic reminders. Many programs teach children to sing a hand-washing song while they scrub their little hands; this makes the procedure more enjoyable and reinforces the correct duration for washing: twenty seconds or longer. Eventually children learn how to wash their hands properly. Model the routine, which should include the following steps:

1. Use warm, not hot water.

2. Wet the child's hands, and place liquid soap (not antibacterial soap) on the palm of one of the child's hands.

3. Away from the water, lather both hands, including the spaces between fingers, under nails, and the back.

4. Continue washing for at least twenty seconds.

5. Rinse hands thoroughly under warm, running water.

6. Dry hands with a clean towel.

You can minimize the pathogens passed from child to child by ensuring that children wash their hands frequently. Make sure they wash their hands at the following times:

- after arriving at the program

- before helping at mealtime

- before and after eating

- before and after playing in water

- after using the toilet

- after touching body fluids: blowing nose, wiping mouth, and so on

- after playing outside

- after playing in sand

- after touching animals

You can minimize your own exposure to or transmission of children's illnesses and those of your coworkers by washing your hands thoroughly at the following times:

- before and after preparing children's meals

- before and after you or the children eat

- before and after changing diapers

- before and after administering medications or ointments if there is a break in the child's skin

- before and after water play with the children

- after using the toilet or helping a child use the toilet

- after touching your own or a child's bodily fluid

- after being outside

- after playing in sand

- after touching the garbage

Cleaning and Sanitizing

Responsive learning environments incorporate routines for cleaning and sanitizing spaces and play equipment into the policies and procedures—that's how central they should be. Use nontoxic, fragrance-free products whenever possible to clean and sanitize toys, floors, and every surface where children eat, sleep, play, and rest. Counters where food is prepared and served must be clean and sanitized. Diapering tables and toilet areas should be sanitized and disinfected according to licensing requirements. Air should circulate freely; rooms should be well ventilated. Monitor and reinforce cleaning and sanitizing practices as carefully as you do hand washing.

Prevention

Ensuring that your environments are safe for young children should be one of your highest priorities. Safety starts with prevention. Make sure your program's policies and procedures specify how to prevent and respond to emergencies so everyone has the same knowledge. Your program should have written guidelines for preventing accidents and illnesses, reporting accidents, creating emergency plans, and carrying out emergency drills for fires, earthquakes, tornadoes, and other natural disasters. These written documents take the ambiguity out of responding to hazards and disasters, and they tell parents that their children will be well cared for during emergencies. Written procedures should include clear descriptions of how parents will be notified and how they can contact your program in case of emergencies.

Be sure that emergency drills include children and staff. Routinely check first-aid equipment, fire extinguishers, and other equipment to verify that they haven't expired. Make sure emergency supplies are easily accessible.

Check indoor and outdoor play equipment and toys regularly to be sure they're safe. Facilities and play equipment should be repaired quickly. Toys that are broken or that pose a safety threat to young children should be repaired or thrown out. Look at your spaces and anticipate unsafe activities that might occur there—then remove whatever could cause them. In other words, do everything in your power to prevent injuries.

You can't prevent all injuries and hazards. Young children are bound to fall, bump their heads, or pinch their fingers. Bumps and bruises are natural parts of growing up. All you can do, or be expected to do, is to cherish and protect your adventurous, questing young charges as well as possible.

Proper Nutrition and Mealtimes

Healthy, well-balanced diets are critically important to growing children. Children burn through calories, and good food is necessary for their physical and mental growth. Providing excellent food to children should start with talking to their families about food and fluid intake, food allergies, and special dietary needs. Such information becomes especially important if children have been ill recently or are starting to show signs of illness. In turn, you should be keeping track of children's eating and drinking patterns in your program so parents can use this information if they need to contact their medical professional. Regular communication between you and children's parents can help both of you support young children's health and well-being.

Infants need to breast-feed or bottle-feed. If you are feeding from bottles, make sure the breast milk and formula are stored and handled properly. Hold babies while you bottle-feed them, and watch closely so you can read their signals. Make sure they can feel the warmth of your body while they feed: this strengthens the secure

relationship you are building with them and helps you respond immediately if they cough, burp, or spit up. The warmth and closeness they feel during feeding tells babies they are safe and loved; they internalize feeding as a pleasant experience, and this association grows when they start to eat solid foods.

Mealtimes for toddlers and twos are lively. They should also be enjoyable and relaxed—never force children to try new foods or to eat at all. They know when they're hungry or full. Model healthy eating and good eating habits by happily trying new foods yourself. Eat what the children eat, and don't consume other foods in front of them.

COMMUNICATION WITH FAMILIES

Part of creating a responsive learning environment is creating partnerships with families. Start this with effective communication between children's homes and the early care program. When you and the children's parents feel good about talking, e-mailing, texting, and phoning each other, you're on your way to creating a highly responsive program. Why? Because steady communication between home and program promotes continuity of care, shows mutual respect, and fosters trust between parents and program caregivers.

You know how vital trust and open communication are, particularly for infants and toddlers, who can't make their needs known very effectively. You need to know what's going on in their homes, and parents need to know what's going on in their children's child care program. You've probably already discovered how widely parents' views vary on healthy and safety issues. You need to respect their views by understanding them fully. If you cannot follow them because of your program's own policies and procedures, be sure to explain this clearly and fully to the family.

Because very young children's needs change rapidly, remember to speak frequently with parents about any shifts they've observed in eating, sleeping, and other patterns—these affect the care you provide. Even short-term changes—for example, a child's having slept poorly the night before—are important for you to know; in this case, you would make sure the child has an additional nap or other down time. Let parents know you want to hear *everything* about their children that could affect their care when they're with you.

Child's Daily Report

Besides your daily conversations with parents, you should make it a program-wide practice to provide families with daily reports on their children's activities while in your care. These reports should include information on how the children ate, how they napped, how often they were diapered, and how you dealt with special health or dietary needs. Cumulatively, such records are useful for tracking children's development and for reassuring families that their children receive continuity of care. (The closing thoughts at the end of the book include more information about working closely with families.)

Records can be filled out on NCR (no carbon required) duplicate forms so you can give one copy to families at the end of the day and put the other in your file for the individual child. (You can order NCR forms locally or from online print companies. These carbonless forms are also useful for accident and injury reports.)

When families arrive for the day, they can complete the top portion of the form, and you fill in the rest of the data throughout the day. You can adapt the form to accommodate infants, toddlers, and twos.

Child's Daily Report

Completed by parent at sign-in:

Child's name _____ Time of arrival _____ Date _____

Name of adult (who signs the child in to child care) _____

Special instructions for the day _____

_____

Time of last feeding or meal _____

Completed by caregiver:

Infant bottle/cup feeding

Amount (ounces)	and	Time of day
_____		_____
_____		_____
_____		_____
_____		_____

Meals

BREAKFAST

What s/he ate _____

How s/he ate her food (well, fair, not so great) _____

Comments (new foods, etc.) _____

LUNCH

What s/he ate _____

How s/he ate her food (well, fair, not so great) _____

Comments (new foods, etc.) _____

SNACK(S)

What s/he ate _____

How s/he ate her food (well, fair, not so great) _____

Comments (new foods, etc.) _____

Diapering or toileting (note time and check appropriate boxes)

Time of Day	Wet	Bowel movement	Runny	Solid	Used toilet (potty)
_____	☐	☐	☐	☐	☐
_____	☐	☐	☐	☐	☐
_____	☐	☐	☐	☐	☐
_____	☐	☐	☐	☐	☐
_____	☐	☐	☐	☐	☐

Napping

Went to sleep at	Woke up at
_____ a.m./p.m.	_____ a.m./p.m.
_____ a.m./p.m.	_____ a.m./p.m.
_____ a.m./p.m.	_____ a.m./p.m.

Caregiver comments

Activities _____

_____

Behavior and mood _____

_____

Problems or concerns _____

_____

Supplies needed

Diapers _____

Wipes _____

Clean clothes _____

Other _____

CURRICULA AND INTEGRATED LEARNING

Responsive learning environments are ones in which children's current interests fuel changes in the curriculum to incorporate those interests. This is often called an *emerging* or *emergent curriculum*, and you probably already implement it, whether you call it by this name or not. If children become fascinated by butterflies, for example, you talk to them about the butterfly's life cycle, read them books about butterflies, teach them songs about butterflies, take them on butterfly hunts, and help them cut out and post photographs of butterflies around the classroom. As long as the activities are age appropriate and hands-on (see chapter 4), young children are going to learn more from pursuing their own interests than yours. An emergent curriculum encourages children to grow and to integrate learning across all four domains.

Observation and Assessment

Observing and assessing the children in your care—along with your own activities—are important to the strength of your curriculum. You can't improve what you're doing if you don't remember what you've done, and you can't repeat successes if you don't keep records of them. The National Association for the Education of Young Children (NAEYC and NAECS/SDE 2003) views assessment as central to the quality of early childhood programs. Here's how assessments benefit you:

- They assist you in making sound decisions about teaching and learning.

- They help you decide when interventions are needed to aid children.

- They help you see where program changes are needed to increase children's learning and development.

Your program may require formal, written assessments, or it may use more informal methods. Like NAEYC, I recommend fully documented assessments because I believe they're likely to track children's milestones, interests, and needs more clearly. They're also easier to provide to families, and communicating children's progress to families, as explained earlier, is key to your program's success.

I see other benefits to using formal assessments and observations. Children who are in care all day often have different primary caregivers in the morning and afternoon. To be highly effective as a child's primary caregiver, you need to know what went on before or after your own time with her. You can use sticky notes or leave phone messages for your coprimary caregiver—some caregivers even use video recorders for their assessments and observations—the medium matters less than the practice. The important thing is to create records that serve the children, their families, and your program well.

Close observation of the children in your care helps you scaffold their activities so they can develop new skills. (I discuss scaffolding in more detail in chapter 2.) Observation is also important as the basis for your written records and your daily communications with parents about their children's progress. It becomes critically important if you notice things in children's behavior that lead you to think they are not meeting their developmental milestones. Discussions with parents and recommendations that their children be professionally assessed should be based on documented observations.

EARLY INTERVENTIONS

Sometimes parents learn very early that their children were born with special needs, and they come to your program knowing and asking for your help with this. But sometimes developmental delays are subtle and don't show up until children are older and have already entered your care. Because the first three years of children's lives are so critical to developing bodies and brains, you must be prepared to assist in interventions as early as possible.

Responsive learning environments can make perceived lags in children's development more evident because of the range of activities and learning styles you support. You should be constantly observing, assessing, and documenting children's growth and development carefully so any possible developmental delays can be addressed. This is an enormous responsibility, and it's yours: you know more about child development than most children's parents; you see a wide range of children in the same age cohort each week; you have the basis for assessing children's development progress. In other words, your observations are invaluable. Make sure that they are thorough and accurate.

If you are concerned about possible developmental delays in some of the children in your care, document your observations scrupulously and convey them as quickly as possible to your program director or appropriate colleague. If a child's delay persists, meet with the parents, tell them your concerns, and listen to what they say about their child. Use your documented assessments and observations and the child's daily reports to show the parents why you are concerned. Encourage the parents to have their child screened by a pediatrician or another health care professional. If a child does need early intervention, offer the family information about the referral process, help them find local programs and services, and support them if a professional assessment is recommended for their child.

INCLUSIVE ENVIRONMENTS

Responsive learning environments incorporate the principles of *universal design for learning* (UDL) into their curricula. These principles were developed by the Center for Applied Special Technology (CAST, accessed 2012) and state that educational programs should provide the following:

- multiple means of representation

- multiple means of action and expression

- multiple means of engagement

Multiple here means that the teaching and demonstration of learning methods and materials are varied to offer accessible learning to all children, whatever their learning style. For example, children can learn about the properties of bubbles by blowing the bubbles themselves, by watching them float, and by making the bubble solution with you. Children can learn about wind chimes by listening to the sounds, feeling the chimes, and watching them move in the wind. If you describe what is happening as the children engage with the chimes or bubbles, you can help children build vocabulary and language skills.

So where does UDL enter the picture? The principles of UDL offer you an expanded range of learning methods and materials so you can reach a wider range of children and are based on neurological research. UDL is not a one-size-fits-all approach. You can apply its principles by providing opportunities for children to explore and engage in the environment both individually and in small groups. Modify and adapt the learning environment to meet the changing needs of all children, which can be as simple as wrapping a rubber band around crayons so little hands can grasp them better. If you notice that some children are sensitive to noise, provide quiet private areas for them to play. UDL can help you create an even more responsive learning environment by making learning a better experience for children across the spectrum of abilities. You can learn more about CAST's work at its website, www.cast.org.

ROUTINES AND TRANSITIONS

Routines are pleasurable to children: they reassure them, provide structure, and ease the transition between home and group care. Routines allay anxiety: like a familiar blanket, they help children feel secure. As children ease into each part of the day, they're surrounded by what they already know and can do. Routines make them calm and relaxed, and once they're calm and relaxed, they're more open to learning, eager to take in new information, and aware of each other and their surroundings. They're ready to assimilate new experiences.

Have you thought about how many routines are part of the day for the infants, toddlers, and twos in your care? Here's a list—probably a partial one—of the activities that provide structure to their days:

Daily Routines That Provide Structure

AGE	MILESTONE		
Infants	• Arrival • Eating • Diapering	• Napping • Hand washing • Teeth brushing	• Outdoor time • Departure
Toddlers and twos	• Arrival • Circle time or story time • Free-choice time	• Cleanup • Snack- or mealtime • Outdoor time • Diapering or toileting	• Napping • Hand washing • Teeth brushing • Departure

When you provide children with routines, you're not only helping them with their basic needs, you're also creating some of their earliest feelings of safety and predictability.

As soon as they understand their daily routines, children start learning about sequencing, and doing so stimulates their ability to remember. They quickly learn their classroom routines and eagerly anticipate what comes next.

In responsive learning environments, routine gets embraced. You talk to the children about what they're doing now and what they'll soon be doing. You link the present to what comes next—for example, you might say, "You're starting to look uncomfortable—do you need a dry diaper? Let's change your diaper, and then we'll go outside to play." Queries like this tell children what to expect; they emphasize the safety and predictability of routines. Greeting children when they arrive or talking with them while their parents leave tells them the same thing: order is being maintained and the home–child care connection endures.

Some children may become upset if the routines they anticipate aren't followed. In responsive learning environments, caregivers understand that children's individual temperaments demand more or less routine, that routines and transitions occur more slowly or quickly, and that you must play a larger role in supporting some children.

FINAL THOUGHTS

Responsive learning environments are central to quality care. The finest programs promote the growth and development of all children. They do so in several ways: by creating physical spaces that welcome families and children and optimize the learning and exploring that can occur there; by ensuring the health and safety of children in care; and by providing daily reports and documented observations and assessments of children's development and activities, which make early screening and intervention more likely if children do not achieve developmental milestones. Responsive learning environments incorporate the principles of UDL so every child's learning style and capacity is supported. Classroom routines and transitions are honored in the belief that they provide predictability and security to young children and prepare them for learning.

WHAT CAREGIVERS CAN DO

- Provide a welcoming space for adults and children.
- Place children's first names and pictures on their cubbies.
- Stock indoor spaces with furnishings scaled to infants, toddlers, and twos.
- Organize rooms to offer a variety of play experiences.
- Design cozy areas away from the noise of busy classrooms.
- Place infants on their backs when they sleep.
- Follow or exceed state licensing guidelines for health and safety.
- Document observations and assessments of children.
- Provide families with daily reports on their children's activities.
- Provide multiple learning opportunities for children.
- Establish and maintain classroom routines.

BIG IDEAS FOR CAREGIVERS

- Quality ECE and care programs should promote the growth and development of all children.
- Good health and safety practices should be continually reinforced in the classroom and the program's policies and procedures.
- Communicating daily with families supports the health and well-being of children.

REFLECTION AND APPLICATION

1. Name three things you can do to design infant, toddler, and two-year-old environments that promote children's growth and development. How would spaces for these different ages differ?

2. How can you use observation and assessment data to improve children's learning?

3. Create a learning plan that incorporates the principles of UDL. How does it benefit all children?

4. Create a plan to improve the routines and transitions of the children you care for. How should you introduce it?

6

Social-Emotional Development: Understanding Self and Others

Social-emotional development is essential to young children's sense of well-being. Their first relationships, those they have with parents and caregivers, teach them who they are and their place in the world. Responsive caregivers help them develop into people with a wide range of social-emotional competencies:

- healthy sense of self
- personal identity
- positive relationships with adults and peers
- self-regulation
- empathy
- ability to care for others
- ability to share

There's so much to learn! These competencies develop out of trusting, nurturing, and responsive relationships. In chapter 3, I discussed the importance of developing secure attachments and the importance of early relationships: these produce emotionally healthy, well-adjusted children. This chapter examines your role in supporting the social and emotional growth of the infants, toddlers, and twos you care for.

Social interactions and emotional development are closely related. Through social interactions, young children form relationships, work to get their needs met, and learn about feelings. They develop emotionally as they learn to identify, regulate, and express their emotions—this is what we mean by the term *emotional development*. The term also refers to children's growing ability to feel concern and empathy for others and their willingness to encourage other people's social and emotional well-being. When you look at social and emotional development, you can see that they're clearly related. For example, children form close and nurturing relationships with caregivers and peers in caring and nurturing social environments. In this type of care, children learn about feelings and emotions and in turn care about others. Because social and emotional competencies develop together, this developmental stage is termed *social-emotional development*. It begins in infancy and evolves throughout people's lives.

INTEGRATING LEARNING

Young children develop their sense of self and personal identity alongside their relationships to adults and peers. During play, they learn to cooperate, regulate their emotions, and show concern for others. When they acquire physical, cognitive, and language skills, they also increase their social-emotional skills. As children grow and their motor skills develop, they are able to physically navigate indoor and outdoor areas and move on their own to seek out friends to play with. With increased cognitive and language skills, they are better able to identify and express their feelings in healthy ways; they learn to communicate their needs to adults and follow simple directions. And they begin to solve problems and use words when they interact with adults and peers.

As a responsive caregiver, you should model appropriate physical and emotional displays for young children. You can rock and sooth a fussy infant or put your arms around a distressed child. You can seat a child on your lap, look into his face, and gently talk with him. Each of these gestures shows care and concern for children who are crying and upset. You should exhibit an equal amount of delight when children behave well. Encourage them to join in activities. Smile and laugh when they're having fun. Encourage them to clap, wave, and smile at their friends and to hug and comfort friends in need. When infants, toddlers, and twos observe these daily interactions and gestures of compassion, they adopt similar behaviors when they form their own relationships with peers.

Toddlers start to play cooperatively once their cognitive and language skills have become adequate. New physical skills, such as riding a tricycle and throwing a ball, offer them opportunities to share and take turns. You can help them grow socially and emotionally by planning activities that emphasize cooperative play. Talk to children about what they and other children are feeling. When you do this tenderly, you promote their social-emotional skills and help them learn how to care for others.

Show empathy for children who miss their families during the day. Some find the transition from home to child care difficult. Offer them love and nurturing while they adjust. They may need more time to make the change when first arriving. You might say, "Sandra is sad because her mommy just left for work. Let's ask her to join us on the rug for a story." Offer children lots of opportunities to develop their emotions and healthy self-expression. Read books and sing songs to them about social-emotional skills—it's a great way to teach them those skills. Display posters of children expressing different emotions. Teach children how to interact positively with adults and peers. Doing so helps them integrate social-emotional development throughout the day.

SOCIAL RULES

Infants, toddlers, and twos begin to learn the rules of society by interacting with other people. Lev Vygotsky believed that adults share their cultural values and beliefs with children through daily interactions (Feldman 2007). Urie Bronfenbrenner proposed that children's beliefs about society and the environment as a whole are strongly influenced by the people with whom they share closest contact, including parents, siblings, teachers, and peers (Patterson 2009). Both theorists understood the importance of teaching young children social rules.

Certain social rules are universally accepted; these are often regarded as common courtesies or politeness. For example, saying "please" and "thank you" are commonly accepted practices. Classroom rules like "We don't hit, bite, or scratch others" are routinely taught in child care settings. Social rules about sharing and not destroying other people's property are commonplace too. For young children, such rules might take the form of not scribbling on another child's artwork or not knocking over a block tower someone else has just built. Remember that children are born not knowing any social rules. It's society's responsibility to teach children commonplace social rules in caring, nurturing ways. You play an important role by passing these rules on to children as well as by respecting families' own and perhaps different beliefs and values.

Help children learn social rules; these provide structure and stability. Express them simply so they're easy for young children to understand and follow. As I mentioned in chapter 2, use positive, encouraging language when you talk with young children. State the rules in positive rather than negative terms. At first, infants won't understand the rules, but they learn in time that rules exist and must be followed in the classroom. Once children reach toddlerhood, they can learn to follow three or four simple classroom rules. Here are some examples:

- Be kind to others.

- Keep your hands and feet to yourself.

- Keep food at the table.

- Ask the teacher for help.

Make these rules part of your classroom's routines, post them with pictures corresponding to each behavior for children to see, and refer to them often. Read books stressing sharing, caring, and saying "please" and "thank you." When you see children behaving in caring ways, acknowledge them with encouraging words: "You and Charlie are playing so nicely together!" or "Thank you for sharing the toys." Strengthen these words with a gentle rub on a child's back or a smile. With your encouragement and positive reinforcement, children quickly learn the rules. As their understanding of rules increases, they become more confident about being able to interact positively with others. Their new confidence helps them build resiliency.

RESILIENCY

Resiliency is the ability to adapt to and survive difficult circumstances. It's a blend of many social-emotional competencies, including developing a strong sense of self, personal identity, close relationships with adults and peers, empathy, caring, and ability to share. Resiliency develops across childhood when children must adapt to the changes and challenges in their lives. Resiliency blooms best in trusting soil: when children have trusting, caring, and nurturing attachments and relationships with adults, they become resilient. In this book, I stress the importance of secure attachments and relationships; these are essential components of children's well-being. When children possess them, they have the necessary tools to become socially and emotionally competent.

Children who lack trusting relationships are less resilient and emotionally more fragile. They may react with greater anxiety and frustration to changes and be more difficult to calm and soothe. Resilient children, on the other hand, feel loved and valued. Trying new things excites them; they are eager to explore new activities. They're flexible, resourceful, and adapt nimbly to changing circumstances. Provide the children in your care with plenty of opportunities to work on resiliency. As they approach their third birthdays, these signs of resiliency commonly emerge:

- autonomy

- self-esteem

- flexibility

- increased ability to communicate needs

- resourcefulness

- imagination

- caring

- empathy

You can promote resilience in young children in several ways:

- **Respond to children's needs in a caring way** Hold a child's hand when she's having trouble walking up stairs.

- **Encourage children's sense of self and personal identity** Acknowledge the child's ability to recognize his own picture on the wall by saying, "That's right, José! It's a picture of you!"

- **Model caring and empathy for others** Respond to a child who has fallen and bumped her knee by saying, "Oh, that must hurt! Who will help me find some ice for her knee?"

- **Provide a predictable, secure learning environment** Teach children classroom rules, such as "Be kind to others."

- **Model positive communication** Verbally acknowledge a child who is sharing his toy by saying, "Thank you for sharing your toy."

- **Promote development of social-emotional vocabulary** Read stories and show children pictures of emotions—for example, *On Monday When It Rained* by Cheryl Kachenmeister or *Richard Scarry's Please and Thank-You Book*.

- **Demonstrate humor and optimism in your attitude toward others** Join children in play and make funny faces and voices when you read to them.

SENSE OF SELF

Providing a nurturing, secure environment helps children develop a healthy sense of self. Humans begin developing their sense of self at birth; it's most deeply affected by early relationships. How people connect, sympathize, and show concern for each other helps define who they are. Those with a poor sense of self may have amazing cognitive or physical abilities, but if they lack empathy and the necessary skills for forming and maintaining healthy relationships, they're unlikely to experience intimacy.

Predictable, responsive environments help young children develop feelings of trust and safety. Children start to believe the world

and the people in it can be trusted. From this foundation, they can build a healthy sense of self.

Social exchanges are important to infants, toddlers, and twos. Gestures like smiling, giggling, eye contact, and facial expressions communicate to and engage them. Infants' social smiles, which begin around three months, are the first evidence of their developing sense of self. Through social exchanges, they become aware that they are separate from others. They wiggle or move their heads to get your attention, and they repeat these actions over and over to keep you engaged. You smile and respond, and they feel joy. This reciprocal action positively reinforces their sense of self.

You can observe young children's healthy sense of self when they joyfully engage in small-group activities. Emotionally healthy children are inquisitive and explore their environments enthusiastically; they move easily from one activity to another and show pride in their actions and accomplishments. When you respond favorably to their social behaviors, you reinforce neural connections in their brains, and they feel safe and secure.

Encouragement is a powerful tool for helping children develop a healthy sense of self. It fuels their internal desire to do their best and sends them the message that whatever they do, they are loved. Encouragement can be as simple as a gentle touch or hug or as complex as offering verbal reassurance such as "You can do it! I believe in you!" or "It was great to see you playing so well with your friends today." Toddlers are delighted by what they can do. Support their feelings of pride by acknowledging their accomplishments. Support their interest in and desire to try new things and complete tasks—you'll reinforce their sense of self and help them build self-confidence. Embrace their emerging sense of self and their efforts to form a personal identity.

PERSONAL IDENTITY

While infants, toddlers, and twos are developing a sense of self, they're also working on a personal identity, a project that continues throughout childhood—indeed, throughout life. Young children try to answer the questions "Who am I?" and "Who am I in the world?" When they're lucky enough to spend time in developmentally appropriate environments, they can integrate their emerging personal identity into other forms of learning. Infants learn to differentiate themselves from others by recognizing and exploring their own faces in the mirror. They learn how to identify their noses, mouths, and ears. You can help them build this awareness by pointing out different parts of the face. Sing songs such as "Head, Shoulders, Knees, and Toes" to help them learn about their bodies and develop a personal identity.

Developmentally appropriate activities help children learn what they do and don't like. They may discover that they enjoy playing with building blocks or painting. When they master putting puzzles together, they gain confidence in their skills.

In pretend play, they learn to act out roles and build relationships with peers. Support children while they're discovering who they are, and help them feel valued and respected.

Children's home cultures influence their personal identities deeply. Understanding their cultures helps you know how to support their emerging personal identities. You should be sensitive to the wishes and cultural practices of children's families and include them in your classroom.

Cultural norms and values are transmitted by families. These can take the form of food, music, clothing, holidays, and religious events. High-quality programs honor children's cultural backgrounds and incorporate their traditions into the curriculum. For example, you can invite a child's family to share their culture's food with the children. You can plan a special day when children wear clothing representing their cultural backgrounds. (I discuss other strategies for partnering with families in the closing thoughts at the end of the book.) By giving families opportunities to share their cultural beliefs and traditions, you can help children develop a personal identity along family lines. You can also integrate cultural practices into everyday activities like music, dancing, ethnic cooking, and literature. Books like *We Are All Alike—We Are All Different* by Cheltenham Elementary School Kindergartners, *Only One You* by Linda Kranz, or *You and Me Together: Moms, Dads, and Kids around the World* by Barbara Kerley introduce young children to a range of cultures.

Gender identity is another component of personal identity. Most children are socialized to be aware of gender roles and gender identity; they internalize what society means in saying, "You are a boy" or "You are a girl." Early relationships strongly identify children's gender identity. Offer children gender-neutral toys and games. Show them books with children and adults in a variety of traditional and nontraditional roles. High-quality learning environments are inclusive and accepting of all children and their families.

RELATIONSHIPS

Children build the foundation of their social-emotional skills on their first caring relationships with adults. Early interactions include facial expressions, smiles, and eye contact. Expressive language, including crying, cooing, and babbling, helps infants engage adults and get their needs met. Children's emotional well-being demands that they form secure attachments and relationships with adults so they can experience trust and autonomy. Caring, nurturing relationships with adults encourage young children to become confident, secure, and resilient.

Relationships with Peers

Infants, toddlers, and twos learn to interact with their peers through social observations and engagement. Infants first watch other infants and may cry when another infant cries. They watch you while you feed and change other babies, and they start to smile and coo at their peers. This is the beginning of their early peer relationships. Older infants face each other on their tummies, smiling and moving their bodies excitedly when they're close to each other. Once they begin to crawl, they move toward other children and may reach for or touch them. Give them opportunities for positive interactions with peers.

Invite older infants and toddlers to sit together on your lap to hear a story. Encourage them to join in small-group activities, sing songs, or play games together. Help them play with each other and build relationships by talking and sharing. You might say, "Please join your friends on the rug for a song" or "It's nice to see Maria and Anthony playing so well together in the playhouse." Toddlers play next to each other at first, watching and listening to their peers. Once their language and cognitive skills become more developed, they start to play cooperatively with peers.

Mealtime is an especially good time for children to interact with each other and form early friendships. They typically enjoy mealtime, where they learn to share, follow simple directions, watch each other, and feed themselves. Meals offer them the chance to smell and taste new foods. Infants who are starting to feed themselves finger foods enjoy sitting up while eating. Small groups of children can sit together to socialize while they eat. Small-group mealtimes encourage young children to observe each other, learn to share, and build relationships. Model each of these behaviors, and scaffold receptive and expressive language during mealtimes. Young children love to help, and mealtimes offer chances for them to serve, pass, and clean up.

Cooperative play emerges when children can take turns, share toys, and build friendships. Other social-emotional competencies (empathy, caring) flower once children open more deeply to their peers. Toddlers and twos are likely to show preferences for certain children. They smile and become excited when they see their friends. Their growing ability to think and speak helps them engage their friends in conversation and play. From age two to three, children imitate others and use their imaginations when they play with peers, deepening their interactions. Their improved ability to control and regulate their emotions helps them form positive relationships.

SELF-REGULATION

Self-regulation is one of the most important social-emotional skills children learn in their first three years. Timing varies from child to child. A child's temperament—easy, difficult, or slow-to-warm—strongly influences her ability to self-regulate. Children need slow, gentle guidance while they're adjusting to new situations. Changes should be introduced gradually, allowing children ample time to move into new activities. Two-year-olds possess new cognitive skills and physical mobility, but their autonomy has limits. They can be joyful and happy one moment, and drop to the floor in the next in puddles of tears and frustration. They may hit and strike out at you and their peers with seemingly no provocation. They're learning social rules about playing cooperatively, and they can easily become frustrated by the limits and rules you set. Try to limit how often you say *no* and *don't* so they don't hear these words too often.

Instead, offer them simple choices that appeal to their growing sense of autonomy: for example, if a child runs through the classroom and you want her to walk, say, "In our classroom, we walk rather than run so all the children stay safe" or "Our outside area is for running. Inside, we walk so all the children remain safe. Do you want to go outside and run?" Acknowledge efforts to self-regulate. Use positive statements: "Thank you for following our class rules" or "I know you want to run—it's fun. I appreciate you walking slowly in the classroom."

Guide children's behavior by giving them clear boundaries and simple reminders about social rules. Spend time on the floor with them; doing so helps you gently guide children whose behaviors are challenging. Protecting their safety is essential. If someone is having a meltdown, guide him to a quiet place and remain with him until he regains composure. If he allows it, you may want to rub his back or stroke his head gently. Reassure him in a calm voice that everything is going to be all right.

Do not shame children or tell them they have behaved badly. Shaming language is very harmful to young children's developing sense of self and personal identity. Remember Erikson's stages of development in chapter 2. Children at this age are moving from the challenges of trust versus mistrust to those of autonomy versus shame and doubt. Encourage children's sense of autonomy and avoid language that shames them like "You're a bad boy for hitting your friend" or "I don't like you when you act that way."

Besides setting limits for young children, you should show empathy and closeness to them. Children who receive loving guidance develop resiliency. You might say, "Tamika looks sad because you took away her bear. Let's find another toy for you to play with so Tamika can have her bear back. It's nice of you to give it back to her. She looks happy now. Do you want to play with the bunny or the dog?" When you provide positive, loving guidance, children feel loved and secure. Their developing sense of self remains intact.

While children are learning about self-regulation, they are also learning to identify emotions and express them in positive ways. They need opportunities to explore the range of emotions they're feeling. Teach them the words that correspond to different emotions when they're calm and relaxed—don't make the mistake of trying to teach them about feelings while they're having a meltdown or crying spell! During periods of emotional distress, they're not emotionally open to learning.

Children who feel physically and emotionally safe and secure are open to learning about feelings. They express their feelings positively. Help all children feel safe, calm, and relaxed before starting a discussion about emotions. You can weave the topic into everyday conversations—for example, when one child hands another a sand bucket, you can say, "Jamie, that was very nice of you to share the bucket with Shawn. Shawn, do you feel happy when Jamie shares? Sharing is a good way to show we care about each other." Books and photos can help children learn about the range of emotions and how to express feelings positively. When children can identify and express their own feelings, they can start to recognize them in others. Their developing sense of self and ability to identify and express emotions moves them along the path toward empathy.

EMPATHY

People who are empathic understand others' feelings and treat others kindly because they know how they feel. Empathy is a complex social-emotional skill. It differs from sympathy, which recognizes but does not engage with another person's suffering or feeling. Empathy is broader and deeper: it develops from concern, compassion, and identification with another's pain.

For children to develop empathy toward others, they must first possess a sense of themselves as separate from others. They must also be able to identify their own feelings. To help children develop these complex skills, use stories and songs that describe children exhibiting empathy and caring to others. Help them build an emotional vocabulary.

Use teachable moments to model and encourage empathic behavior. For example, say, "Oh, you fell down and bumped your knee! I'm sorry you hurt yourself. Let's put a bandage on it" or "It looks like Billy's feeling sad. Let's go give him a hug to cheer him up." Infants and toddlers may show distress when other children become upset and express empathy by looking worried and motioning to you to help the distressed child. A two-year-old might go up to a sad or upset child and offer a hug or a toy to comfort her. When children's language and social-emotional skills become more highly developed, they solve problems and seek assistance to aid other children who are upset.

CARING FOR OTHERS

Children learn to care for others while they are developing their own sense of self, personal identity, and empathy. Once they learn to recognize their own feelings and emotions, they start to see them in others. Initially, they care by mirroring the caring behavior of others. Caring gestures (smiles, laughs, gentle touches, hugs) tell developing children how to care for each other and reassure them that they are safe, secure, and loved. Everyday moments of thoughtful caring transform how children see themselves in the world.

Sharing

Learning to share is another important childhood task. Adults often expect young children to share naturally, but this isn't an easy skill to acquire. Some toddlers share without being asked, whereas others need plenty of time to learn. Sharing takes practice to master. Toddlers are still striving to get their own needs met and are only starting to recognize the needs of others. Usually by the time they turn four, they have learned to share and take turns. These skills help them once they start to play cooperatively.

Don't punish or use shaming language when children are learning to share. Explain how to share and why it's good to take turns. Demonstrate how to share a toy and say, "Thomas has the toy now, and then it will be Shawn's turn." When children find it hard to share, give them the words they need and encourage them to ask the other child to share: "Kayla, you look like you want a turn with the drum. Ask Mickey to give you the drum when he's finished. Say, 'Can I have the drum when you're done?'" As children's speaking skills improve, they become better at sharing and playing cooperatively.

Children need plenty of opportunities to practice social-emotional skills. Talk with them about what sharing is and why it's important. Offer them chances to share and take turns throughout the day. At mealtime, ask them to pass food and take turns setting and cleaning the table. At circle time, ask them to take turns helping you read a story or passing a beanbag or scarf during a song. Outdoors, ask them to share tricycles and balls and take turns on the slide. To minimize conflict, provide enough toys and objects and carefully monitor popular items so everyone can play with them.

Carefully observe and document children's social-emotional growth over time (see my discussion in chapter 5). No absolute indicators of developmental delays exist. The Centers for Disease Control and Prevention (CDC 2012) identifies social-emotional behaviors that should be evident in children by their third birthdays:

- appropriate eye contact

- warmth or joyful expression

- sharing or enjoyment

- recognition of own name

- playing pretend games

- playing with others

If you notice that some children do not display these behaviors by age three, document your observations and meet with their parents to discuss what you've seen. Developmental delays should be discussed sensitively and clearly so parents understand your concerns. If infants or toddlers show signs of developmental delay, encourage families to have their child screened by a pediatrician or another health care professional.

FINAL THOUGHTS

Developing social-emotional skills is essential to the well-being of young children. Their relationships form the foundation for understanding and caring for themselves and others. They develop these skills through play and other social interactions with adults and peers. They become resilient when you encourage and model positive behavior. Create an atmosphere of trust and security in which social-emotional skills can develop. Social-emotional competencies include positive sense of self, personal identity, healthy relationships with adults and peers, self-regulation, empathy, caring for others, and ability to share. Your relationships with young children are critical to their developing these competencies. They develop these skills in part through physical activities, and you can enrich these with my companion book, *Activities for Responsive Caregiving: Infants, Toddlers, and Twos,* which describes activities that support social-emotional development in young children.

WHAT CAREGIVERS CAN DO

- Respond to babies in loving and caring ways.
- Tell babies how special and loved they are.
- Sit with babies and help them identify their facial features by looking in a mirror.
- Acknowledge children's gestures of empathy and caring for others.
- Post simple rules and corresponding pictures about classroom behavior.
- Talk with children about their feelings.
- Read books about feelings and emotions.
- Use expressive language when talking with children.
- Use encouraging words throughout the day.
- Stay calm when children have meltdowns.
- Avoid the words *no* and *don't*; restate negative behaviors positively.
- Give children who are having difficult days extra care and love.
- Encourage small-group activities so children can build relationships with their peers.

BIG IDEAS FOR CAREGIVERS

- Social-emotional competencies develop from trusting, nurturing, responsive relationships.
- Resilient children are flexible, resourceful, and able to adapt to changing circumstances.
- Responsive caregivers give children chances to share and take turns throughout the day.

REFLECTION AND APPLICATION

1. How do you model caring behavior in your classroom?
2. Name three teaching strategies and three activities that foster infants', toddlers', and twos' social-emotional skills. How do these strategies differ for infants, toddlers, and twos?
3. How can you modify your caregiving to meet the social-emotional needs of each child?
4. How can you further your knowledge of social-emotional development?
5. How do you plan for a child who shows delays in developing self-regulation and empathy?

Physical Development: Sensing and Moving

Children develop physically at warp speed in their first three years. They start as infants who can't hold up their own heads, and in no time at all they're two-year-olds who can run, jump, and ride tricycles. Newborns spend most of their days sleeping and eating and are completely dependent on adults. By the time they're toddlers, they have learned to sit up, crawl, walk, and feed and dress themselves. Toddlers and twos are in constant motion, using their newly refined gross- and fine-motor skills to explore the world. Along with their physical development, infants, toddlers, and twos develop perceptual (seeing, hearing, smelling, tasting, and touching) skills.

Children's physical abilities become more refined with age; their perception and awareness increase. They integrate new experiences more efficiently and understand the world better. Perceptual and motor skills develop in tandem with other learning domains. You see this in a two-year-old who leaps up, points at the sky, and cries out, "Miss Emily—look! I see a butterfly!" The child is demonstrating his developing language, cognitive, perceptual, and motor skills, all at once. In the first three years, children need plenty of sleep, healthy food, room to explore, objects and materials to play with—and most of all, plenty of love. Love is the glue that holds the whole package together. It encourages the young child to trust his senses and to trust himself.

Jean Piaget believed that from birth infants are trying to make sense of the world through sensory perception and motor activity. He called this period of development the *sensorimotor stage*, and it lasts from birth to about age two. Piaget thought infants' knowledge of the world is limited to their sensory experiences and motor activities and that these drive their cognitive development.

He observed that adults play important roles in children's sensorimotor development and their ability to acquire new cognitive and physical skills. The gentle, nurturing care of adults is essential to the growth of infants, toddlers, and twos if they are to progress to the next stages of childhood. Learn to respond to children's sensory and motor needs and experiences. For example, when you hand an infant a toy, make sure that its surface is textured and brightly colored so the child can explore the surface with her mouth and see its color. If the toy makes a sound when she shakes it—all the better. A simple toy can offer her plenty of opportunities to develop and integrate her sensory and motor skills. Provide the widest possible range of materials and objects to stimulate young minds, young senses, and young muscles.

PERCEPTUAL DEVELOPMENT

Perceptual development is the term used to describe the ability to perceive the world through the senses. Children from birth to age three acquire mastery of their senses rapidly, absorbing sensory impressions from everything around them. They learn from what their senses tell them.

Babies are born with sensory systems ready to see, hear, and interact with the world. When they nurse or are given a bottle, they taste and smell the milk and feel the warmth of the person holding them. They see your face and the pattern of your blouse. They hear you talking or singing to them. Each new phase of their development brings new opportunities to expand their perception of the world.

In early care programs, young children experience a perceptual world different from the one at home. They hear a variety of adult voices, the hum of lights, many children laughing and crying, the sounds of music and singing. They learn that indoor and outdoor areas offer different perceptual experiences. Provide the link between home and early care for infants with continuity of care: work with parents to honor young children's schedules and preferences. By providing predictability and consistency, you and the children's parents create environments that reassure children so they feel confident enough to explore new sensations and savor new stimuli.

Observe very closely to see if children are becoming overstimulated. Remember that initially their world is almost wholly one of sensations. Some children are very sensitive to touch or sound; they may cry, fuss, or stiffen if new or too many stimuli are present. Other children tolerate and even seek out more stimuli; they may cry and fuss when they're bored and want to be stimulated. Understand the children in your care, and respond to the level of sensory experience each child wants. Modify or adapt the environment for them. For example, if an infant becomes fussy or starts to cry indoors, you might suspect there's too much noise and stimulation in the room. You might take him outside, sit quietly, and rock him until he calms down. Learning how each child perceives the world and responds to sensory stimuli is one of your important responsibilities.

The early care environment plays a critical role in children's sensory experiences and integration. As their brains grow and develop, some sensory data become hardwired. They use what they have learned to make sense of newer information. When a

child has learned his rattle makes a sound, he shakes it. When he is given a different rattle, he learns that the new one looks, feels, and sounds different from the old one. He's learning to discriminate between rattles on the basis of his sensory experiences. High-quality early care offers a variety of sensory experiences to young children to encourage perceptual development and integration of the senses.

Vision

Newborn babies' vision is not fully developed. Although they can see, their vision is blurry. This changes over the first several months. Infants from birth to three months quickly learn to track faces and objects and smile when they see familiar faces. By three months, they can see objects clearly. You can help them train their eyes by placing them on their backs under an infant activity gym or on an activity mat so they can see and touch the soft objects hanging above them. Between three and six months, they start to use their feet to move the objects hanging from mobiles. They are fascinated by objects that move gently in the wind; they become infatuated with overhead fans. They start looking at their hands and feet, and they put them in their mouths. By six months, their vision is fully developed, and they reach for familiar objects and enjoy experimenting with rattles and other objects that make noise. They continue to show a preference for human faces, including their own. You can give babies three months and older toys with shatter-resistant mirrors on them or put a mirror on the wall near the floor so they can see themselves. These activities enrich their perceptual development and help them connect their experiences, sense of self, and the real world.

Provide infants and toddlers with a variety of objects to see and explore. You can create a soft felt book with pictures of the babies in the classroom or display their photos on the walls. When you show infants and toddlers new things, identify each of them by name. You might say, "Look at the flower. It's yellow. It has petals on it. Shall we look for the watering can and water the flowers?" Indoor and outdoor environments offer children different things to see. Remember that they're all novel to young children. When they see the colors and patterns on a butterfly's wings for the first time, you should be excited, too, because you've introduced them to the wonders of the world. Once infants learn to sit on their own, then roll, crawl, and walk, they acquire more opportunities to experience and manipulate their environment. They begin moving on their own toward desired objects and people.

Hearing

Infants' auditory systems develop in utero and are fully operative at birth. Babies have decided preferences for human voices and turn their heads toward their mother's voice immediately after birth. Newborn babies prefer the pitch and sound of adult voices over other sounds. They can discriminate between adult's and children's singing, and they prefer to hear adults sing songs meant for children (Patterson 2009). Once they can hold up and turn their heads from side to side, they know where sounds come from and can make sensory connections between what they see and hear. You can help them develop this skill by holding them in your arms or sitting with them on your lap outdoors. Babies can hear the different sounds the wind makes, the tinkle of wind chimes, the *whoosh* of a windsock. Infants exposed to the sounds of adults talking, reading out loud, and singing soon learn to discriminate the sounds of language. Introduce music and songs into their environment, and allow infants and toddlers to explore musical instruments while they listen to their sounds.

Learning to listen is a skill essential for forming sounds and words and acquiring language. (I discuss language development further in chapter 9.) Observe how infants respond to sounds. If you have any concerns about a child's hearing, share those concerns with parents, and recommend that their child be assessed by a health care professional. Hearing is a critical milestone in perceptual development.

Smell and Taste

Like hearing, smell and taste are well developed at birth. Babies can distinguish their mothers by smell alone. They also seem able to be able to differentiate among sweet, salty, sour, and bitter flavors (Patterson 2009). They prefer sweet smells, show preference for sweet tastes like breast milk, and smile when sweet-tasting liquids are placed on their tongues. When they're exposed to bitter or sour tastes, babies wrinkle their noses and exhibit distaste (Feldman 2007). When new foods are being introduced, infants' reactions are purely sensory: they respond to smell, taste, temperature, and texture. Vegetables smell and taste different than fruits or cereals. Meat has a texture very different from that of fruits or vegetables. These new sensory experiences may or may not be pleasurable to infants. Notice their responses, and introduce new foods slowly. Children between six and ten months can signal their preferences and let you know if they want more or are finished eating.

Touch

One of the most important and highly developed sensory systems in newborns is touch. Skin-to-skin contact, in which babies lie between their mothers' breasts or on their fathers' bare chests, allows them to use adults' body warmth as an incubator. Newborns respond favorably to skin-to-skin contact; it helps them form secure attachments to their parents. Skin-to-skin contact has been used as therapy for premature babies to promote their survival. Skin is the largest organ of the human body, and it's highly reactive when touched, rocked, cuddled, and soothed. It sends critical messages to the brain about trust, pleasure, security, and their opposites.

You play a critical role in helping mothers and infants form secure attachments, as I discussed in chapter 3. One of the ways you support these attachments is by providing nursing mothers with quiet areas where they can breast-feed. Skin-to-skin contact during nursing reinforces feelings of love and safety for babies. You provide similar contact when you hold a baby next to your face or gently stroke her face. Understand and make use of the importance of touch; be sensitive to children's need to be held, rocked, and touched lovingly.

High-quality programs offer infants, toddlers, and twos many sensory experiences. Children discover that materials and surfaces feel different from each other, so encourage touching by offering children many different textures. Help them learn what to call these surfaces (*rough*, *smooth*, *bumpy*, *sticky*, and *soft*). Be sensitive to their sensory likes and dislikes—some children find touching certain surfaces or textures distasteful. Modify environments to meet their sensory needs.

GROSS-MOTOR DEVELOPMENT

Gross-motor skills involve the large muscles of the body that empower walking, sitting up, kicking, and similar functions. Children develop these motor skills gradually. Development norms are recognized, but some gross-motor skills, such as walking, are commonly acquired over a fairly wide range of months. As children grow, their bodies and movements become more refined. Developing more complex gross-motor skills goes hand-in-hand with learning to observe the world from a variety of positions. Infants spend a lot of time on their backs and stomachs, viewing the world from the floor up. They learn by first moving their arms and legs and turning their heads toward familiar people. This early activity develops their gross- (large-) motor muscles so they can soon sit unassisted, crawl, pull themselves up, and then walk.

Learning to Sit

By three months, most babies can prop themselves up on both arms and lift their shoulders from the floor. By four months, their drive to see the world better gives them more control over their bodies: they start rolling over. When they reach this developmental milestone, never leave them alone on high surfaces. Babies practice rolling and spend a lot of time on their backs, playing with their feet and kicking their legs. These activities strengthen their muscles and prepare them to sit up unassisted at around six months. Start checking the environment for dangers they may encounter when they start exploring on their own. Make sure you have safety locks on all electrical receptacles, that electrical cords are kept out of reach and cannot be pulled or moved, and that objects are safely secured so nothing can fall on wandering infants.

Sitting without help requires balance and muscle strength. While they're learning to sit unassisted, babies may assume a tripod position, with one hand placed on the floor for balance. The other hand may reach for a toy, or they may roll onto their backs and play with the toy they've just reached. When they begin reaching for objects while sitting, they often tumble and roll. Getting back into sitting position is their first step in becoming mobile. They soon realize that they can scoot or creep on their tummy or bottom. Sitting, scooting, and creeping soon lead to balancing on hands and knees. Before you know it, they're crawling—the next stage in their physical development.

Crawling

Crawling offers babies a highly improved form of mobility. Now they can use both sides of their bodies in coordinated fashion to move speedily. At first, infants crawl by balancing on their hands and knees. They may rock back and forth. Once they begin to push off from their knees, they're crawling. Some "bear crawl" by using their hands and knees while keeping their buttocks in the air.

Crawling is an exciting time for babies. They need lots of open space to practice their new skills safely and plenty of room to explore and discover the world. You can kneel a few feet away and encourage them to crawl toward you. You might say, "Look at you crawling! Can you crawl over to me? I see you crawling to me!" Provide crawling infants with lots of opportunities to move around indoors and outdoors. Create play centers filled with toys and manipulatives for them to use. Outdoors, you can provide soft rugs and pillows for them to sit on, and shade to protect them from the sun. Be certain that all toys and objects are in good repair and aren't too small for crawling infants. Check the floor throughout the day, and remove any items that could cause infants to choke. Because they put so many items in their mouths, they're at high risk of choking.

Crawling typically begins between six and ten months. Not all infants crawl, though the majority do. When you observe an infant of six to ten months who is not beginning to crawl, this may be a sign of a developmental delay. You should discuss your concerns with the child's parents. At this point, the child may need to be assessed by a health care professional.

Pulling Themselves Up

Around eight months, sitting and crawling have strengthened most infants' legs, buttocks, and stomach muscles sufficiently so they can pull themselves up to standing positions and start walking. During this phase, babies crawl to a table, sofa, or chair and pull themselves up. Using the furniture to steady themselves, they quickly learn to move around it. This is a great time to offer them push toys and wheeled playthings to help them gain balance and confidence in their new ability to stand and walk. Their first unassisted steps are exciting for babies and adults. At first, they take a few steps, squat to pick up a toy, and then stand up again, unassisted. Their muscles are stronger and their coordination improved. Provide them with low, sturdy furniture and bookcases for stabilizing themselves. This is a wonderful time to introduce soft climbing structures so they can continue to develop their gross-motor skills.

Walking

Babies learn to walk across a fairly wide range of ages. Most begin walking around twelve months. At first, they may be a little unsteady, but with practice, they start walking freely. While they're still learning, they often stumble and fall. Keep a close eye on them at all times and quickly comfort any child who falls. By sixteen months, children should be walking with ease. This means they can navigate from room to room, climb up and over furniture and stairs, and begin using their large muscles

to ride and push toys. Walking soon turns into running, climbing, and jumping. By eighteen months, children typically can climb up and over raised platforms, walk while carrying items, and begin using small riding toys. Soft climbing structures and wood or plastic play structures offer them opportunities to practice climbing. Many of these structures include slides, which toddlers enjoy. You can help them learn how to go up and down a slide safely by holding the sides with both hands.

FINE-MOTOR DEVELOPMENT

Fine-motor skills develop when children can control the small muscles and movements of their hands and fingers. Infants and toddlers first use these movements to grasp and manipulate objects with their whole hand. You can encourage fine-motor development by providing infants with things to reach for, including rattles and soft toys. With practice, their fine-motor skills become more refined. Toddlers develop their fine-motor skills further by feeding themselves, playing with blocks, stacking rings, and digging in the sand. Two-year-olds use their fine-motor skills to play with puzzle pieces, draw with crayons, and manipulate playdough. As children develop more strength and dexterity in their fingers and hands, they can manipulate and explore objects more closely and skillfully.

Reaching for Objects

Infants can grasp and reach for objects when they're born. You see this in newborns who wrap their entire hand around the fingers of their mother or father. This grasping reflex helps parents make early emotional connections with their newborn. The grasping reflex disappears at about two months, and the baby's fists, clenched until now, open up and start reaching for objects. *The search is on!* When infants can grab mobiles, rattles, or baby bottles, they start to learn more about their environment. Provide them with infant activity gyms or activity mats so they can flap their arms or swipe at objects to make them move or make contact with them. Even more important, infants at this stage use their new ability to reach out in order to touch your face or play with the buttons on your shirt. They are connecting with you as well as exploring the world through their senses.

At four months, infants become more skillful in their ability to hold and reach for objects. Their new fine-motor precision coincides with their ability to recognize and locate desired objects, toys, or people. It's part of their growing cognitive skills. Infants use their hands, arms, legs, and feet to reach out. They hold things against their bodies and open and close their hands.

Give them opportunities to practice reaching and grasping by placing interesting objects in front of them. By five or six months, babies can reach out, grab objects, and start to shake and hold them. With practice and access, they become more skilled at reaching and holding objects, including their bottles. These first stages soon morph into more complex manipulations. As soon as infants notice that toys make sounds and can be moved, they start to see them as objects of interest and delight. Toys that offer varied textures, sounds, and moving parts appeal powerfully to babies and help them integrate sensory stimulation and motor activity. They also help them increase their cognitive skills. Finger and hand muscles become stronger and capable of greater precision when infants reach and play with toys. Soon they can grasp and manipulate small items with a pincer grasp.

Pincer Grasp

Infants start by picking things up with their entire hand. As they grow older and their skills become more refined, they use a pincer grasp—that is, they form a circle with their thumb and index finger and pick things up between the two. Once they've learned to coordinate this movement, they can feed themselves small pieces of food. They can also push, spin, and turn the knobs on toys. Between six and seven months, infants typically begin to transfer their toys from one hand to the other and reach in all directions while they're sitting alone. At this point, you should offer them manipulatives like stacking rings, beads to string, large puzzle pieces, and chunky pegboards so they can develop their fine-motor skills and hand-eye coordination. Once they can sit up unassisted, they enjoy scooping things into containers and rolling balls. As their fine muscles grow and become more controlled, infants become skilled at feeding themselves and using utensils.

When children approach their second birthdays, they're becoming quite independent. Their sense of autonomy flowers, along with their "Me do's" and "I do it myself's." Encourage and support toddlers and twos in their quests to discover and do things on their own. Scaffold their learning and show patience for their developing skills. For example, here's how you might help a child who is just learning to feed herself and having trouble using a spoon. You can gently place the spoon in her hand and guide it toward her mouth. You can encourage her efforts by saying, "Look at Tonya using her spoon! You're feeding yourself. Tonya, you're doing it all by yourself!"

Toddlers and twos need a variety of materials and toys to play with while they're fine-tuning their ability to grasp and manipulate objects. Older toddlers and twos show interest in using pencils, crayons, and scissors. Although their fine-motor skills aren't yet refined, they're starting to scribble, draw, dress them-selves, and fasten clothing. During their first three years, they increasingly use the new strength of their fingers and hands to manipulate objects and become independent.

UNDERSTANDING THE MILESTONES

Children reach developmental milestones at different ages. Some children reach one milestone early and then take longer to reach the next. Some children skip over one skill altogether, like crawling: some babies simply stand up and start walking instead. It's not unusual to see some children regress just before they develop new skills. Remember that every infant, toddler, and two is unique; each develops and masters skills in a singular way.

But there are milestones and then there are milestones. Observe the children in your care regularly and carefully, and document their growth and development. If they aren't meeting developmental milestones or moving along the development continuum, discuss your concerns with their families. Early detection of de-

velopmental delays helps families get the interventions they need for their child's optimal learning. For example, if a child isn't crawling or beginning to pull himself up between six and ten months, you should recommend that he be evaluated by a health care professional.

Here's a guide to the developmental skills that are recognized in the field of child development. Use the list to determine if infants and toddlers are meeting their developmental mile-stones. Note the overlap in age ranges for the skills. These reflect the range within which children commonly reach the individual milestones.

Milestones of Physical and Motor Development

GENERAL AGE RANGE	MILESTONE	
Birth to four months	• Tastes, hears, smells, and touches • Sees; vision blurry but improves • Cries to communicate needs • Smiles at adult • Makes eye contact	• Lifts head to look around • Swats mobile • Grasps small objects like rattles • Tracks faces and objects
Three to six months	• Reaches for objects • Swipes at mobile • Looks at and plays with hands and feet • Holds baby bottle • Lifts head from lying position	• Pushes upper torso off ground using shoulders and hands • Rolls over • Uses tripod position • Sits unassisted
Six to to ten months	• Rocks back and forth on hands and knees • Crawls • Pulls up to standing position • Pushes and pulls wheeled toys	• Uses pincer grasp • Feeds self finger foods • Picks up and manipulates simple toys
Nine to thirteen months	• Crawls, scoots, and creeps • Holds books and looks at pictures • Plays with stacking rings • Strings large beads • Plays with large puzzle pieces	• Places chunky pegs in holes with assistance • Scribbles • Begins to roll balls • Begins to dress and fasten clothing
Twelve to twenty months	• Begins walking; still unsteady • Moves around room • Sees objects and moves to play with them • Shows preferences for smells and tastes	• Stacks toys • Opens and closes objects • Moves push-and-pull toys around room • Places items in containers • Uses spoon to feed self
Eighteen to thirty-six months	• Walks with ease • Climbs small number of stairs • Climbs up and over low platforms • Walks while carrying items • Transfers items from one hand to other • Rides small riding toy	• Plays with small puzzle pieces • Uses playdough • Paints at easel • Colors with crayons • Starts experimenting with motions of writing

FINAL THOUGHTS

Children's physical development changes rapidly in their first three years. Young children learn about the world by sensing, moving, and exploring. Their sensory skills include seeing, hearing, smelling, tasting, and touching. They develop their

perceptual skills through sensory experiences. My companion book, *Activities for Responsive Caregiving: Infants, Toddlers, and Twos*, includes many activities that provide sensory experiences.

Gross- and fine-motor skills typically develop over time. Children's large muscles develop as they learn to sit up, crawl, pull themselves upright, and then walk. You should provide developmentally appropriate environments that allow children to explore and develop their large muscles by crawling, climbing, walking, running, and jumping. Toys and objects support gross-motor development and should include toys for pushing, pulling, and riding. While their large muscles develop, infants and toddlers also acquire fine-motor skills. At first, they can only reach for objects. As their fine-motor skills become more refined, children move from using their entire hand to reach and grasp objects to feeding, dressing themselves, and grasping crayons and chalk to draw.

Because children reach developmental milestones at different ages, you should carefully observe and document their growth over time. Discuss any concerns you have about possible developmental delays with parents as soon as possible. Encourage them to have their child assessed by a health care professional. Early intervention is essential so children can reach their developmental milestones without significant delay.

WHAT CAREGIVERS CAN DO

- Provide infants with rattles and objects that move.
- Provide infants with a variety of sensory stimuli.
- Encourage children to use their motor skills (rolling, scooting, crawling) to obtain objects.
- Provide soft objects for children to crawl over and through.
- Provide low tables and sturdy, low furniture for children to hold while they're learning to pull themselves upright.
- Provide materials for scribbling and drawing.
- Provide small riding toys.
- Show children how to push and pull objects.

BIG IDEAS FOR CAREGIVERS

- Perceptual and motor skills do not stand alone—they are uniquely linked to other learning domains.
- Listen to and observe how children integrate sensory information. Then adapt your teaching strategies to their needs.
- Newborn babies are equipped with sensory systems ready to see, hear, and interact with the world.

REFLECTION AND APPLICATION

1. Name three things you can do to increase physical development in your classroom. How should the environment differ for infants, toddlers, and twos?

2. Name three strategies and activities you can use to develop perceptual, gross-motor, and fine-motor skills in young children. How should these strategies differ for infants, toddlers, and twos?

3. How can you address the needs of children who show signs of physical delays in their development?

4. What two things can you do to further your knowledge of physical development?

Cognitive Development: Thinking and Learning

Cognitive development begins at birth, when infants start to make sense of the world. Everything is new to them. They're smelling aromas, tasting foods, hearing sounds, and feeling textures for the first time. With each new experience, the brain makes neural connections. (I discussed this in detail in chapter 4.) High-quality learning environments provide a variety of ongoing experiences that strengthen these connections in infants. As they are reinforced, the brain is strengthened and cognitive skills increase. You can offer children from birth to age three experiences that help them develop their cognitive skills. By the time they reach their third birthdays, their ability to think, reason, and solve problems will have grown remarkably, thanks to the exposure to new things you've given them.

Cognitive development isn't a simple, step-by-step process. Young children develop cognitive skills by integrating a variety of underlying skills. These increase alongside developing motor and sensory abilities. For example, infants' and toddlers' sensory perceptions and motor activities help them explore and discover the people, things, and events around them. A toddler who decides to play outdoors in the sandbox might see a shovel and a sand bucket and begin to scoop sand into the bucket. When the child recognizes that the bucket is full, she will probably pour out the sand and start filling up the bucket again. She is using her sensory, motor, and cognitive skills as she scoops the sand, pours out the sand, and thinks about repeating the

process. She can feel the sand on her hands and watch the sand spill out of the bucket. By encouraging child-directed, developmentally appropriate activities, you can help young children build their cognitive skills to better understand how the world works.

Jean Piaget believed that children are naturally curious and construct their own learning through trial and error. They test their own theories about the world and build on their existing knowledge. As I discussed in chapter 2, Piaget viewed cognitive development as a series of stages during which children confront core challenges. He believed that children from birth to age two develop their cognitive skills through sensory exploration and motor development; he called this the *sensorimotor stage*. During infancy and toddlerhood, children learn through exploration, trial and error, and repetition. Everyone's seen infants and toddlers repeat motor activities, like pushing buttons on toys or putting objects into boxes and then removing them. It's clear they're trying to understand what they're dealing with and that they're learning the properties and functions of these objects as they explore them. As they're exploring, they're also making new neural connections. Once children's cognitive skills have increased, they understand the properties of objects better. When they move into what Piaget termed the *preoperational stage* (ages two to six), they start to understand what Piaget called *object permanence* and *mental representation*.

OBJECT PERMANENCE

Understanding object permanence is a cognitive milestone for infants. Piaget observed that children under eight months believe objects disappear as soon as they aren't visible or can't be heard. Sometime between eight and twelve months, infants start to understand that people and objects exist independent of them. They grasp the concept that out of sight or hearing doesn't mean out of existence. Mastering

this concept starts when babies realize that objects exist even when they can't be perceived. The game of peekaboo is a case in point: infants who have not yet grasped the concept of object permanence believe that when an adult covers her face with her hands, she has disappeared. As their ability to grasp the concept of object permanence increases, infants happily engage in the playful game by pulling away an adult's hands to reveal her face. They know you're still there behind your hands, even when you can't be seen.

Once infants understand object permanence, their ability to find hidden objects soars, and they delight in finding objects hidden from their view. This major milestone is a great time to start playing games like hide-and-seek. You can also show infants small toys and then hide these behind a pillow. Together, the two of you search for the objects to see if you can find them. Once infants have mastered how the game is played, they start hiding objects for you to find. (I provide many activities in my companion book, *Activities for Responsive Caregiving: Infants, Toddlers, and Twos,* that you can use to help increase children's cognitive skills and teach them object permanence.) Once they've achieved mastery of the concept, infants and toddlers can start creating mental representations of images and concepts.

MENTAL REPRESENTATIONS

Mastering object permanence helps children understand symbols, the basis of creating mental representations. Mental representations are mental pictures of objects, people, places, and ideas. Piaget believed that children start to develop schemata and symbols to represent objects between eighteen and twenty-four months. Schema become more complex as children become more efficient thinkers. Children eight to twelve months can create mental images of balls when asked to think about balls, but their images lack properties. Once children have acquired more experience by playing with balls and learning their various properties, their mental images of balls become more detailed: balls have colors, textures, and bounce or roll. These more

complex internal images help children expand their play and develop more complex cognitive skills.

Mental representation helps children think, reason, and solve problems. When they can hold mental images in their heads, children can retrace their steps to look for lost objects. They can follow simple directions, build new objects, and expand their play activities. They can act out situations and behavior they have observed. Toddlers might pretend to feed or rock a baby doll, retrieving images of how to do so from what they've seen at home or school. Mental representations also provide structures for pretend play. In these and other ways, children draw on their memories of symbols, images, and concepts. (Although images and concepts are considered different forms of representation than symbols, they, too, demonstrate children's increasing cognitive abilities.)

As they explore and learn about objects, children discover their properties; for example, a bead is round, and a cube has six flat sides. They develop mental representations of objects and their properties. Their brains store this information, which can be retrieved later to solve problems or follow directions. Suppose, for example, you ask a child if she wants to string beads. If she has already played with beads and stringing laces, she knows what you're asking her to do because she possesses a mental image of beads and what it means to string them. She also has a mental image of the basket that holds the beads and laces and where it can be found.

As children's store of mental representations increases, they can master more complex tasks, like sorting and categorizing. Remember that they're developing these cognitive skills along with receptive and expressive language. Help them connect their growing store of mental images and symbols to words. Books containing photographs of real objects help reinforce mental images.

CAUSE AND EFFECT

Another cognitive skill that infants start to learn very early is cause and effect. Initially, babies seem surprised when a toy moves or makes a noise. They may look at you for reassurance and try to read your response to this surprising event. Their own explorations of cause and effect are simple at first: they swipe at a mobile or shake a rattle, and something happens. When they repeat the action, they may accidentally use a different part of their bodies and produce a different reaction. Through trial and error, they run through a variety of gestures to elicit the desired response. Each of their attempts generates a cognitive connection in the brain. When they become more mobile, they test their theories by making more elaborate cause-and-effect attempts. Does a wooden spoon make the same sound when hit against the floor as when it hits a soft pillow or a plastic toy? Infants learn cause and effect by exploring, pure and simple. They push, pull, twist, and rotate objects to understand their properties better. Toddlers might build a tower from soft blocks and use their problem-solving skills to see if the opening in it is large enough to drive a toy car through. High-quality early learning environments encourage young children's hands-on, play-based explorations of cause and effect.

Infants experience cause and effect when they start cooing and babbling, and you coo and babble in return. This reciprocal exchange reinforces their efforts. Cause and effect also fuels infants' social-emotional development. Cause-and-effect

explorations support infants' perceptual development too. Babies learn about objects through their senses, observing how they work, what sounds they make, how they open and close. Interactive toys with buttons to push and objects that spin or light up reinforce cause and effect and perceptual development.

Children's problem-solving ability increases when they can experiment with cause and effect by taking things apart, putting them back together, and manipulating objects. As their thinking develops, toddlers become more intentional in their explorations. They discover that they can put toys in a plastic shopping cart, and then they wonder: *What else can I put in the cart? And where can I go with it?* They might fill up the shopping cart with books and soft toys and wheel it outside to play.

MEMORY

Piaget observed that children develop mental pictures, or schema, through trial and error, and use this prior knowledge to construct new knowledge. They store this information in their memories, from which it can be retrieved to create more advanced thinking and reasoning. As their attention spans grow, they can retrieve a wider range of information and play with objects longer; this is why they outgrow toys and books and demand more challenging ones. Recognize the growing complexity of a child's brain and the importance of creating learning environments suited to different developmental stages.

Responsive early learning environments are designed to help children build memory skills. They provide routines and structures that give children opportunities to predict what happens next and that build on existing memories. Share what is going to happen throughout the day with children. In the morning, tell them what the day's activities will be. Tell the toddlers or twos, "Today, we're going to play indoors and outdoors. We'll sing songs and read books. There are puzzles and beads for you to play with too. It's going to be warm today, so I'm going to put out the water table for those of you who want to use it. I'll put out yellow paint, paintbrushes, and sponges for you to paint with." At the end of the day, talk with the children about what they did and what activities will occur tomorrow. Routines like these offer continuity, security, opportunities to follow simple directions, and memory exercises.

You can promote language and cognitive development by asking open-ended questions and scaffolding language development. Help children recall information from past experiences and connect it to present activities and events. Talk with them throughout the day about the people and objects in the books you're reading, the food they eat for lunch, the toys they enjoy. Such interactions strengthen children's memories, language, and cognitive development.

IMITATION

Long before infants understand themselves as separate people, they can imitate the facial expressions and hand gestures of their parents and caregivers. Children as young as six weeks can imitate the facial expression of strangers (Meltzoff and Moore 1997). Infants have been observed matching gestures like sticking out their tongues to those of adults. They also self-correct imitative gestures to better match those of adults.

These games that babies play are the foundation of later imitations. All play? Not really: Imitation is how cultural knowledge and family ways get passed down. Infants and toddlers learn their families' cultures by watching and mimicking people around them. The better they are at imitation, the more thoroughly they are imbued with the cultural values and practices of their families.

Connect imitation to language and vocabulary. Young children happily imitate sounds and repeat the words they hear. You might say, "This is a turtle. Can you say *turtle?*" They respond by saying the word *turtle*. You smile and say, "That's right! *Turtle!*" Take the time to speak slowly and repeat words. Learning songs and playing with musical instruments increases language development by linking words to imitative gestures. Children learn songs from fingerplays like "Itsy, Bitsy Spider" and by watching and imitating you.

When their cognitive skills improve, children can integrate memory, mental representations, and symbols into imitative gestures and behaviors. In dramatic play, for example, a toddler might mimic a phone conversation he's observed at home. He imitates his father's gestures by nodding his head, frowning, and pretending to listen to someone on the phone. He might shake his head "no," or he might shake his finger at a doll.

When infants and toddlers become more experienced at manipulating objects and remembering their properties, they can imitate those objects' actions and sounds. The properties of things reside in a child's memory and can be retrieved to solve problems or engage in pretend play. For example, you read a book about farm animals to a small group of children. While you read, you demonstrate the sounds each animal makes. The children repeat and imitate the sounds, and because their memory is now developed and supple, they can easily retrieve the sounds when they see representations of farm animals. They might play with toy animals or see photographs of them independent of the book you're reading, and they can reproduce the sounds they heard when you read to them.

SPATIAL AWARENESS

Infants become aware of space very early. Spatial awareness is the ability to understand the position of objects in relation to other objects. After their first few months, infants can see more clearly, and they begin to observe how people and things move. They might watch the objects on a mobile flutter and change direction when they touch each other. When they explore objects with their mouths and move or manipulate toys, they learn about spatial and sensory properties. Through trial and error, they learn how items fit together or open and close. As they get older, they may play with puzzle pieces or soft blocks.

Provide child-directed activities, toys, and objects so infants and toddlers can learn about objects in space. Play mats provide them with objects that move and rotate and teach them about spatial awareness. Not only do children learn about the spatial properties of objects, they also learn about their own bodies in space. As they become more mobile, offer them interesting things to crawl through and over, including pillows and climbing tunnels. These objects provide hands-on learning about how their bodies fit, or don't fit, into spaces. Acknowledge children's efforts to navigate space and use language and verbal cues to support their growing awareness of space. You might say, "Miguel, I see you crawling through the tunnel. Can you crawl over to the mirror?" When you introduce new toys and objects to them, very young children start to see these things in relation to other objects. They use this awareness to solve problems; for example, how to move around other objects and where a new toy is in relation to other toys. Such experiences teach children how things move and how they are related to other objects.

MATHEMATICAL AWARENESS

Young children develop mathematical awareness when they learn to identify, group, and categorize objects. Once they begin exploring the world through their senses, they soon start to categorize and sort what they find. For example, they quickly learn which toys make sounds and which ones roll or bounce. Later mathematical awareness includes a child's developing sense of numbers.

You can encourage number awareness in your daily interactions with young children. For example, you might say to a baby, "You have two beautiful eyes and one beautiful nose" or "Let's put your shoes on. You have two shoes. Here's one, and here's the other." You can also introduce number awareness through songs, games, and stories. Songs like "Five Little Monkeys Jumping on the Bed," "Head, Shoulders, Knees, and Toes," and "Hokey Pokey" teach children new words, music, rhythms, and categories of body parts. Books like *Brown Bear, Brown Bear, What Do You See?* by Bill Martin, Jr., *Ten Little Fingers* by Annie Kubler, and *Colors, ABC, Numbers* by Roger Priddy help children make connections between objects in the books, categories of objects, and number awareness. With practice, children soon become more proficient at classifying objects into groups.

Categorization is a key component of mathematical awareness for infants, toddlers, and twos. As their language skills develop, they become more skilled at categorizing and learning about the smaller sets of similar objects we call *subsets*. They learn to categorize dogs as animals that are different from other animals such as cats, cows, and horses. Later, they learn about a small subset of dogs that have brown, tan, or black fur. Their learning moves from simply defining dogs as animals to describing them in greater detail. Once their vocabulary expands, they might identify dogs as *big, brown, with curly fur and pointed ears*. At this stage, their number awareness is also increasing, making such categories as *big* and *little, more* or *less,* and *some* or *more*

possible. These conceptual terms help children describe things more accurately. Although they may not fully understand the value of numbers, they start to recognize different categories and smaller sets, or subsets, of things. When you ask a toddler, "How old are you?" she may hold up her fingers and say "Two" or "Three." Although she knows the word *two*, she doesn't really understand the relationship between holding up two fingers and her age. In this case, it's easy to see that cognitive development is very closely linked to the child's developing language skills.

Being able to sort, group, and make connections between like or similar objects prepares children for more complex math skills. In play-based learning environments, children acquire the foundations for math skills through the activities you provide.

You can scaffold their learning by offering similar objects for children to sort, including large and small wooden beads or same-sized beads in different colors. Objects of different sizes provide toddlers with opportunities to apply the concepts *big* and *small*. Sorting cubes give them the chance to sort items by shape and color. You can set up a sensory station where children can explore a variety of scents, such as lemon, rose, lavender, and peppermint. Encourage them to talk about the scents and identify the ones they like or dislike. Ask them to describe occasions when they smelled the scents before and why they like or dislike them. This helps them integrate learning across domains and commits children's experiences to memory.

CONNECTING EXPERIENCES TOGETHER

Infants and toddlers constantly build new knowledge, memories, and representations. As their cognitive skills increase, they start to connect these more effectively.

The more children experience, the more neural connections they make. Piaget was convinced that young children use their natural curiosity to construct views of the world. High-quality early learning environments stimulate children's natural curiosity so they want to understand their own experiences.

Responsive caregivers play important roles in helping young children build on existing knowledge and make new connections. Talking and reading to children are key strategies for building their vocabularies and connecting what they observe and experience to words. Use props like puppets to help children make connections to stories and make reading engaging and fun. Activities with music, hand gestures, and body movements encourage children to build connections through sensory experiences. Plan a variety of developmentally appropriate activities that help children connect many kinds of learning.

FOLLOWING SIMPLE INSTRUCTIONS

As children's skills in receptive and expressive language and mental representations increase, they can begin to follow simple directions. When you ask them to put their toys on the shelf, they first need to understand clearly what a shelf is and to possess a mental image of placing their toys on that shelf. They learn to follow directions when you help them build on their existing knowledge of directions. Model the task, and walk children through your directions, step by step. Once their memories and

mental representations have increased, three-year-olds can follow two- or three-step directions.

You can use picture-and-word charts to help toddlers and twos learn simpler directions. Images help them see what steps they need to follow. For example, a Now-and-Then chart might provide pictures of children eating (*now*) and going outside to play (*then*). These charts help children follow simple directions and learn a sequence. As their language skills improve, they can follow directions better. Keep your initial directions simple, and use language that children understand. They need sufficient language skills and cognitive understanding to be successful at following simple directions. These are skills they'll need in preschool. Be patient while they're learning to follow directions, and scaffold their learning by modeling the desired behavior.

FINAL THOUGHTS

Children develop cognitive skills by exploring the world. Their ability to think, reason, and solve problems increases as they integrate learning across the developmental domains. Neural connections become strengthened when children master concepts of object permanence and mental representation. Two developmental tasks of early childhood are integrating learning and developing complex thinking skills (for example, cause and effect, memory, imitation, spatial and mathematical awareness, connecting experiences, and following simple directions). Offer children opportunities to learn about the world and the creatures and objects in it. (My companion book, *Activities for Responsive Caregiving: Infants, Toddlers, and Twos*, provides activities that support cognitive development in young children.)

WHAT CAREGIVERS CAN DO

- Play games like peekaboo with babies to help them learn object permanence.
- Talk to children about what they're seeing and experiencing.
- Read books with photographs of real objects to children to reinforce their mental images.
- Provide objects like rattles for infants to play with so they learn about cause and effect.
- Follow classroom routines and schedules so toddlers and twos can predict the day's activities.
- Retell stories and ask children open-ended questions to help them build their memories and mental representations.
- Provide objects for children to sort and categorize.
- Provide props and objects for children to use in pretend play.

BIG IDEAS FOR CAREGIVERS

- Cognitive skills increase when young children build on their prior knowledge.
- Babies begin to understand object permanence when they learn that people and objects continue to exist even when they cannot be seen, touched, or heard.
- Mental representations help children develop language, cognition, and social skills.

REFLECTION AND APPLICATION

1. Name three things you can do to help children build cognitive skills.

2. Name three teaching strategies or activities you can use to develop cognitive skills in infants, toddlers, and twos. How do these strategies differ for infants and toddlers?

3. How can you integrate cognitive development across other learning domains?

4. What two things can you do to further your knowledge of cognitive development?

Language Development: Playing with Sounds and Using Words

Infants are born ready to interact and communicate with others; they are born ready to learn and use language. Even before they have the physical and mental abilities to interpret and speak words, they are attentive to them and other human sounds. Learning to use language is one of the universal tasks of children from birth to age three, and you play an important role in making this process possible and pleasurable for them. In this chapter, I discuss the roles adults play in supporting children's speech, the best practices you should use in your program, and when you should intervene in delays in children's language acquisition.

ACQUIRING LANGUAGE

Every language has its own set of sounds, tones, and speech patterns. Infants are born with the amazing ability to hear the subtle sounds of all the world's spoken languages. In fact, they have the ability to learn any language. The sounds, tones, and patterns of speech an infant hears set the stage for acquiring a specific language. You play a critical role in scaffolding language development through listening, speaking, and reading to the infants, toddlers, and twos in your care.

Many children in the United States come to child care programs with a home language other than English. Programs may have specific policies for supporting infants and toddlers who are dual-language learners; that is, children who are learning two languages simultaneously. Caregivers who speak the child's home language may choose to use both languages when speaking and reading to the child. Sometimes parents of dual-language learners prefer that caregivers speak only in English to the child, because the parents will speak the home language with the child at home. Whatever your program's policy on dual-language support, infants and toddlers who are exposed to two languages simultaneously will indeed learn both languages.

First- and second-language development occur in the same part of the brain. Like all children, dual-language learners develop both languages through talking, reading, singing, and play-based oral-language activities. Developmentally appropriate environments provide learning experiences that enhance both first- and second-language development. It's critical that you talk with the infants, toddlers, and twos in your care. Use props such as puppets and photographs of real objects to introduce and reinforce new vocabulary. Sing songs, read books, and tell stories. Children learn first and second languages by hearing them—so you must talk with them!

STAGES OF LANGUAGE ACQUISITION

Language involves a give and take of words and gestures. This give and take, often called *serve and return*, provides children with experiences to develop their language skills. You can have conversations with infants who can't yet talk by simply mimicking their vocalizations. Infants and toddlers with good hearing acquire language in the same sequence worldwide.

Receptive Language

Before eighteen months, infants chiefly use receptive language—that is, they mostly listen to and understand what they hear rather than speak. In one sense, they're similar to adults who learn English as a second language (ESL): ESL students and infants both start by becoming proficient listeners and only later speak aloud the words and sentences they already understand. Babies are different from ESL learners: they lack the muscle control to form words and the cognitive ability to recognize the relationships between language and the concepts, objects, memories, and mental representations that words refer to.

Babies listen to the language that surrounds them. Positive interactions such as reading, singing, and talking exposes them to words and sounds. Their attentiveness and reactions to the voices and faces of familiar adults are their first steps toward acquiring spoken language.

Expressive Language

Before they can speak, babies cry to express their needs for food, warmth, companionship, and physical comfort. As their bodies mature, they expand their expressive language to other sounds, gestures, and facial expressions. Infants smile and wiggle, and soon make sounds other than crying to audibly express their feelings.

Cooing is the first stage of language development. Infants start to coo at about three months. They repeat vowel sounds like *aaaaaa*, *oooooo*, and *eeeeee*. These sounds are formed at the back of the throat. Cooing is common when infants and adults play together. If adults coo enthusiastically in response to infants' sounds, babies eagerly continue to coo. They throw in other expressive language too: facial gestures, body movements, and eye contact.

Babbling comes next. This starts around six or seven months, and it builds on cooing. Now infants use consonant-vowel combinations (*goo goo, ba ba ba*). Once babies start babbling, they cycle enthusiastically through a wide variety of combinations. Parents are delighted, of course, because two of these combinations are *da da da* and *ma ma ma*. Babies are no fools: these combinations clearly delight their primary caregivers, and eventually infants assign these sound clusters to the people who respond so enthusiastically to them. Such positive exchanges reinforce infants' efforts to continue exploring and using sounds.

Adults often use a type of speech with young babies called *parentese* (PBS, accessed 2011). Parentese isn't baby talk: it doesn't use nonsense syllables and primitive grammar. Instead, parentese is highly inflected, using raised and lowered tones in a sing-songy way. Real words are used, and sentences are short and simple. Highly animated facial expressions and gestures accompany parentese and signal adults' delight. The give-and-take of parentese encourages babies to use language; it tells them how important language is to adults.

Spoken Language

Children's first recognizable words typically are spoken between ten and fourteen months. These words name real objects and familiar people—words including *blanket, bottle, baby, mommy,* and *daddy.* At first, children's words may consist of shortened forms (for example, *ish* for *fish, itty* for *kitty,* and *da* for *daddy*) and can often be understood only by adult caregivers or the child's siblings. These solitary, often mispronounced, words must stand in for entire requests or statements, and misunderstandings between the toddlers who utter them and the adults who hear them are common. Toddlers can become very frustrated by their inability to make themselves understood. They throw themselves into language, becoming animated and accompanying their words with expressive language (exaggerated hand and facial gestures), and still they can be misunderstood.

By the time they're twelve to fourteen months, most children have much greater command of words and are no longer so frustrated by language. At this point, they start to use words when they play. They may pick up a soft block and pretend it's a phone; they say, "Hi. Bye" and hang up the block.

Vocabulary develops quickly once children reach about eighteen months. Sentence structure develops more slowly. At first, children connect words in two-word phrases; these expand quickly to longer constructions. Toddlers and twos don't grasp verb tenses, plurals, or subject-verb agreement; they say things like "My feets are wet."

SUPPORTING CHILDREN'S ACQUISITION OF LANGUAGE

Language is dynamic; it's a give-and-take between two or more people. From birth, infants understand that language is directed to them, and they listen and watch for it attentively. As someone who spends hours each day with babies, toddlers, or twos, you can support their acquisition of language by listening, speaking, singing, and reading to them. Look for opportunities to scaffold their emerging language skills. Once they start acquiring words, build their vocabulary by asking open-ended questions and modeling social use of language.

It's become commonplace for adults to ask children to "use your words." This may be an unrealistic expectation: if children already possess the words, they use them. When an adult asks a child to "use your words" instead of his physically expressed anger or frustration, this, too, may be unrealistic, because young children are unlikely to understand their emotions well enough to substitute words for feelings. Don't pressure young children to use language. Instead, offer them a safe, nurturing place to practice and build language skills.

Help infants and toddlers develop language skills by talking to them throughout the day. Tell them what you are doing while you feed, diaper, and play with them. Use your interactions to shower babies with a variety of words and sentences. Toddlers and twos can sing songs and listen attentively to stories. When they begin talking, they eagerly join you in give-and-take conversations and songs. As their language skills improve, you can encourage them to play dress-up and make-believe, which stimulate speaking during role playing.

Years of observing young children have taught me that supporting infants' use of language rests on this simple foundation:

- Respond enthusiastically to infants' gestures.

- Mimic babies' cooing and babbling.

- Pause and take turns when talking to infants.

- Read and sing to babies.

- Expose babies to a variety of sounds.

- Vary and play with your voice when you talk to babies.

Best practices for developing toddlers' and twos' language are similar:

- Engage children in give-and-take language exchanges in which they talk and you listen.

- Be patient when children start to explain their needs.

- Avoid finishing children's sentences for them.

- Talk to children about the events of the day.

- Identify and name new and familiar objects for children every day.

- Ask open-ended questions, and give children time to respond.

- Use conversations and story time to build vocabulary.

- Provide daily opportunities for reading, singing songs, chanting, and fingerplays.

USING CONCEPT WORDS

Toddlers' growing vocabularies reflect their surging cognitive growth. At this stage, they're developing their understanding of concepts like cause and effect, time, and space. You can help them attach words to abstractions by using concept words regularly. For example, you might start by stressing simple words such as *inside* and *outside* when you explain where to put away toys at the end of the day. Here are some concept words that help young children learn not just concepts and vocabulary but relationships:

- over
- under
- around
- through

- in
- out
- between
- together

USING SONG, RHYTHM, AND RHYME

Playing with sounds, songs, and rhymes engages children in language and builds the foundation for future reading. Infants' first exposure to songs is usually lullabies. Every culture has songs its members traditionally sing to babies. These gentle tunes help calm and soothe infants, lull them, and build associations in babies' minds between pleasure and words. So does being read to on an adult's lap: children learn to associate books and words with warmth and pleasure.

Babies, toddlers, and twos enjoy learning songs and nursery rhymes. At first, they don't understand the words, but they delight in singing and playing with the words. Traditional childhood songs and nursery rhymes like "Row, Row, Row Your Boat" and "Hickory Dickory Dock" give young children plenty of chances to play with language and blend sounds. Playful spoken language strengthens their love of language and sets the stage for emergent literacy.

Older babies enjoy picture books with silly, made-up words and rhymes: *Moo, Baa, La La La* by Sandra Boynton; *Click, Clack, Quackity-Quack* by Doreen Cronin. Songs that incorporate language, body movement, and fingerplays, including "Itsy, Bitsy Spider" and "Pat-a-Cake," develop children's language and motor skills simultaneously. When songs stimulate children's gross- and fine-motor muscles as well as their vocabulary, children get a thorough—and thoroughly enjoyable—mental and physical workout!

USING PRINT

Young children learn much of their vocabulary and the rules of language from books and other print. *Dialogic reading* is the term used to describe reading in which children are actively involved: they ask and answer questions about the story, turn the book's pages, and retell the story in their own words. When they're actively engaged in these ways, they acquire language more easily and pleasurably. Dialogic reading stimulates children's vocabulary and helps correct language errors. Best practices recommend that you read to children at least fifteen to twenty minutes each day.

The physical nature of the books you read to children are initially as important as the stories those books tell. Infants like cloth books and chunky books that their clumsy little fingers can easily handle. They enjoy mouthing books and exploring them with their senses. Younger toddlers enjoy books that are word free and full of pictures; these encourage imaginative storytelling and many interpretations. Once children are about eighteen months old and expanding their vocabulary rapidly, they seem to enjoy books containing photographs of real objects that they can learn to identify by name. Books that offer simple text and large print, such as *The Very Hungry Caterpillar* by Eric Carle, engage children who are close to learning to read.

It's impossible to reread a favorite book to children too many times. Repetition is soothing to young children; it also gives them the chance to recite along with you, demonstrate what they've learned, show off their I-know-what-comes-next. They enjoy picture books, stories that rhyme, and ones with plenty of repeats. (My companion book, *Activities for Responsive Caregiving: Infants, Toddlers, and Twos*, contains a list of recommended books for infants, toddlers, and twos.)

Don't overlook the print that can be found in everyday life: road signs, restaurant menus, the words on cereal boxes. Such environmental print is likely to be among the first encounters children have with printed words. You can augment such signage by labeling every area of your classroom—for example, "Art Area," "Library Area," and "My Family."

ADDRESSING DIFFICULTIES IN LANGUAGE ACQUISITION

Babies, toddlers, and twos who are engaged by language listen to the words and sounds around them. If a baby doesn't respond to you when you speak, look into your eyes when you address her, or react to loud noises, these may be signs that she has a hearing impairment. Because language is acquired within such a compressed period, it's critical that children who have difficulty hearing be evaluated and treated as soon and as early as possible. When children can't hear language, they lose the capacity to hear; their brains prune it away in favor of other senses. If you notice that a baby isn't responding to your voice or to loud noises in typical ways, refer her parents to a health care provider immediately. Early exposure to words and other sounds are prerequisites to language, so advocate as passionately as you need to get children the help they need.

Developmental Delays

Every child develops language abilities at his own rate, but failure to meet certain developmental milestones is cause for concern. Infants who show no interest in expressive language or whose pitch, intonation, rhythm, or voice quality is irregular or odd should be evaluated by a pediatrician or other health care professional (First Signs 2012). Screening and speech therapy can move children with developmental delays toward language competency.

FINAL THOUGHTS

Language acquisition is one of the principal tasks of children birth to age three. Initially, they use gestures to express their needs, but they listen to the people around them from birth, busily making the neural connections that form the basis for eventual speech. During this critical period of language development, give-and-take between caregivers and infants is essential. Responsive caregivers should speak slowly and pause to listen to children's responses, nurture children's efforts to use language, and talk, sing, and read to children throughout the day. Programs that are language and print rich encourage children's acquisition of language. Hearing impairments and developmental delays interfere with children's ability to acquire language; when either is suspected, it's critical to notify parents and begin early interventions.

WHAT CAREGIVERS CAN DO

- Respond enthusiastically to babies' gestures.
- Read a wide variety of books to children.
- Listen to what children say, and respond to them.
- Help children connect words to objects.
- Follow children's interest in print materials.
- Play with sounds and rhyming words.
- Sing and use nonsensical, silly words.
- Talk to children about the day's events.
- Ask children open-ended questions.

BIG IDEAS FOR CAREGIVERS

- Promote early language development by talking with young children throughout the day.
- Use intentional language, and help young children connect words to real objects.
- Plan language-rich environments so children can build vocabulary and enjoy playing with sounds and words.

REFLECTION AND APPLICATION

1. Name three things you can do to expand the use of reading, singing, and print in your daily activities.
2. How do you respond to infants' early vocalizations?
3. How does responsive care affect infants' language development?
4. Name three things you can do to develop language skills in young children. How do these strategies differ for infants, toddlers, and twos?
5. How can you further your knowledge of language development?

Closing Thoughts: Becoming a Responsive Caregiver

High-quality early learning environments are essential to the healthy growth and development of young children. Every high-quality program starts with responsive caregivers who care for infants, toddlers, and twos, partner with families, ensure secure attachments and relationships between adults and children, and assist children in acquiring skills across the four learning domains.

Not surprisingly, those of you who attain these demanding goals—and do so with joy and commitment—are firmly grounded in your knowledge of early child development, your own professional development, and your partnerships with colleagues and parents. (So important are your relationships with parents that the National

Association for the Education of Young Children [NAEYC, accessed 2011] spells out caregivers' need to communicate openly with families.)

Here, then, is my summation of who you responsive caregivers are, what you have already accomplished, and what you need to do next.

PARTNER WITH FAMILIES

Parents are children's first and most influential caregivers. Partner with children's parents, and support them in their roles. Remember that for children to develop socially and emotionally, they must form secure attachments with their parents. Secure early attachment to parents or other parent figures builds a healthy foundation for young children: it enables children to form other healthy relationships later in life and gives children resilience.

Help parents learn as much as possible about their children's development; provide them with information on how children learn across the four learning domains. Remind parents that children are active learners who acquire skills at different rates. Share information with them through newsletters, conferences, face-to-face conversations, e-mail—whatever it takes to keep the conversation going. Recommend books and articles that parents might want to read. Offer families self-guided exploration-and-discover activities that children can undertake at home. Keep parents informed about free parenting workshops; consider hosting some, and offer child care during events at no charge. Assemble a lending library with books on child development and parenting that families can borrow.

Children are better engaged in learning when their parents participate in their education. Encourage family members to volunteer in your classroom. When they do, give them meaningful work to do. Structure volunteer activities so they don't become economic burdens for parents. Working parents may find it difficult to spend

time in the classroom; perhaps they can help instead at evening events. With sufficient notice, they might be able to volunteer in the classroom or for a special event. Ask them if they can occasionally stay for a few minutes at drop-off or come early at pickup to read stories to the children.

Communicate daily with families on their children's progress. The child's daily report is a convenient way to document children's development for you and their parents to review. Use it so parents can learn what their children do and feel connected to their children's activities. You and the parents can use the report as a basis for discussing children's daily activities and documenting any concerns you or they have.

Always remember that open communication, mutual respect, and clear understanding of what's in the best interest of the child characterize healthy parent-caregiver partnerships (NAEYC, accessed 2011). If your program receives federal funding, as Early Head Start does, be sure you fully comply with government regulations on parent involvement and parent-caregiver partnerships.

Remember that high-quality programs welcome family members, view cultural diversity as an asset, and value children's ties to their family and its culture. Children learn best in environments that value their home cultures. NAEYC (2009) states that children are more likely to learn easily when their caregivers understand cultural differences and honor children's family culture. You should also strive to preserve children's attachment to their home languages.

How can you do this? You might honor children's home cultures by planning activities that highlight their home languages, cultural beliefs, and practices. You might plan a week of special programming during which families share music and food from their home cultures. This is a terrific way to draw families into your program's activities and show your respect for them. Older toddlers and twos can participate in planning and sharing family cultural events. Invite families to use the event to teach their children more about their own backgrounds. If they join your planning process, you can expect a high level of involvement all around.

COMMIT YOURSELF TO CONTINUOUS PROGRAM IMPROVEMENT

Always look for ways to improve the learning environment and the interactions of children in your care. Understand the concept of universal design (I discuss this in chapter 5) and how it applies to children's differing learning styles. Familiarize yourself with the *Infant/Toddler Environment Rating Scale*, revised edition (ITERS-R), and the *Family Child Care Environment Rating Scale*, revised edition (FCCER-R). These scales rate infant/toddler and family child care learning environments. Indicators of quality include organization of space, interaction, activities, schedule, and provisions for parents and staff (Harms, Cryer, and Clifford 2006, 2007). Use these assessment tools to improve the quality of your care environment. Monitor the health and safety of your facility regularly—*and always put the needs of the children first.*

High-quality programs survey families at least once each year to learn what they think needs improving. You might query families about their satisfaction with hours

of operation, communication with caregivers, health and safety, and family support services. Improve your program by responding positively to parents' feedback. Design and carry out a plan to improve the quality of your program—and make sure it includes professional development.

Training in early childhood education keeps you fresh by acquainting you with new strategies for caring for young children. Training programs should include infant and toddler development, intentional teaching strategies, first aid, and observation and assessment. High-quality programs send staff members to training on the warning signs of developmental delay and designing inclusive learning environments. Make sure you also update yourself regularly with training on the signs and symptoms of child abuse/neglect and your role as a mandated reporter of abuse and neglect.

Your program should provide time for you to redesign your learning environment to meet the changing interests and needs of young children. Time for intentional planning, observation, and assessment should also be given priority. Meetings with colleagues should include ample time for discussing daily schedules, activities, and improving care. Hold yourself to examining and improving every aspect of the care you provide.

FINAL THOUGHTS

Because more infants, toddlers, and twos now spend most of their weekdays in the care of people other than their families, the need for high-quality early care will keep growing. I know you take your responsibility to provide such care very seriously: it amounts to a sacred trust. Commit yourself to developing and maintaining the highest quality program. Equip yourself with knowledge of early brain development, temperament types, and developmentally appropriate practices. Because you know better than anyone else that infants, toddlers, and twos learn through play, provide the children in your care with small group sizes and child-directed activities. Support

continuity of care so children feel secure and form healthy attachments.

Your role in in the lives of infants, toddlers, and twos makes a tremendous difference to their growth and development. Become the best responsive caregiver you can—you're essential to children's growth and well-being. By providing optimal care, you point young children confidently down the path toward happiness and well-being.

WHAT CAREGIVERS CAN DO

- Regularly set time aside to meet with parents.
- Partner with parents to support children's home culture.
- Survey parents annually about their satisfaction with the program.
- Create a program-improvement plan.
- Modify your program to meet the changing needs of families and children.
- Offer parenting resources and workshops.
- Set goals for your ongoing professional development.
- Discuss the needs of children and families regularly with colleagues.

BIG IDEAS FOR CAREGIVERS

- High-quality care emphasizes partnerships between families and the early care program.
- High-quality early learning programs are committed to continuous improvement.
- High-quality early learning programs hire highly qualified employees.
- High-quality programs give caregivers time to redesign learning environments to meet children's changing interests and needs.

REFLECTION AND APPLICATION

1. Name three things you can do to partner with parents to promote high-quality care for infants, toddlers, and twos.
2. How can you support the linguistically and culturally diverse backgrounds of children in your care?
3. Design a plan for your ongoing professional development.
4. Name three things you can do to integrate learning across the domains.

Glossary

ambivalent attachment: A type of parent-child emotional tie in which a child is unsure if his parent will protect or provide for him. A child with ambivalent attachment may exhibit a mixture of clingy and avoidant behavior in the parent's presence.

attachment: John Bowlby's theory that parent-infant interactions produce emotional ties. Bowlby believed that quality of attachment forms the basis for a child's capacity to feel secure and form trusting relationships throughout life.

avoidant attachment: A type of parent-child emotional tie in which a child does not seek out a parent for comfort or security. The child does not believe that the parent will protect or provide for her. This child does not cry or seem upset when the parent is absent and avoids proximity to the parent.

axon: A long, strand-like fiber at the end of a neuron that passes information to the dendrites of other neurons.

caregiver: Any adult besides the parent or guardian who cares for a child for any length of time.

child's daily report: An account of a child's day given to a parent by a caregiver. The report typically includes information about how the child ate and napped and how often he was diapered. It also includes information about how the caregiver dealt with special health or dietary needs. These records are useful for tracking a child's development and for reassuring a family that the child is receiving continuity of care.

cognitive development: A field study in neuroscience that focuses on a child's intellectual development. Cognitive development includes a child's increasing ability to process information, conceptualize, perceive, use language, and so on.

cognitive development theory: Jean Piaget's theory that a child is actively engaged in her own learning. His theory suggests that a child is a little scientist, who tests her theories (through play, for example) on how objects work and connects new learning with what she already knows or believes.

concept word: A word that denotes a cognitive concept such as cause and effect, time, or space.

concrete operational stage: The third stage of Jean Piaget's theory of cognitive development. This stage generally occurs between the ages of seven and eleven and is characterized by a child's appropriate use of logic (such as in classifying or viewing things from another person's perspective).

dendrite: A short, branched extension of a nerve cell along which impulses are received from other cells.

developmental competencies: A continuum of skills, learning, and progress typically observed in young children across the developmental domains.

developmental delay: A child's failure to meet certain developmental milestones typical for his age.

developmentally appropriate practice (DAP): A perspective in early childhood education whereby a caregiver nurtures a child's social-emotional, physical, and cognitive growth. Following DAP, a caregiver bases all practices and decisions on (1) theories of child development, (2) a child's individual strengths and needs, which are uncovered through authentic assessment, and (3) a child's cultural background as defined by his community, family history, and family structure.

developmental milestone: A marker or guidepost that enables parents and professionals to monitor a child's learning, behavior, and development.

dialogic reading: A form of reading in which a child actively participates. The child might ask and answer questions about the story, turn the book's pages, or retell the story in her own words.

disorganized attachment: A type of parent-child emotional tie in which the child does not shape his behavior around the parent. The child's behavior can appear bizarre and random; his actions and reactions to his parent are incongruent. A child exposed to traumatic events, including severe abuse, neglect, and isolation, is the most at risk for developing disorganized attachment. He finds forming close, loving relationships with others challenging.

early intervention: A process used to recognize developmental delays in children and to initiate early actions to address them.

ecological systems theory: Urie Bronfenbrenner's theory that child development is an ecological system through which a child develops relationships across multiple settings and over time. This model consists of four levels or systems: microsystem, mesosystem, exosystem, and macrosystem.

exosystem: A level in Urie Bronfenbrenner's ecological systems theory in which a child interacts with a wide community, including her neighborhood, extended family, and parents' work environments.

expressive language: Any form of communication that helps an infant engage an adult to attend to her needs. Expressive language includes crying, cooing, and babbling.

failure to thrive: Revealed by symptoms such as a lack of interest in surroundings and a failure to grow, gain weight, or reach developmental milestones.

fine-motor skill: A skill that relies on a child's small muscles, such as the ability to hold materials, turn knobs, and snap buttons.

formal operational stage: The final stage of Piaget's theory of cognitive development. This stage—achieved during adolescence or adulthood—is characterized by abstract thinking.

glial cell: A cell that supports neurons by providing a myelin sheath to coat the axons.

goodness of fit: How well a child and caregiver relate to each other and to the nature and demands of the environment.

gross-motor skill: A skill that relies on a child's large muscles, such as crawling, sitting, and walking.

home–school connection: The relationship between the people at a child care setting and a child's home.

A strong connection is built on trust and a shared commitment to provide the best for the child.

independence skills: Also known as a self-help skills, these are skills related to taking care of oneself, such as feeding, toileting, and dressing.

learning environment: A setting in which learning takes place. Learning environments should support children's diverse temperaments and stages of development and incorporate the principles of universal design so every child's learning style and capacity is addressed.

least-restrictive environment: Identified in the US Individuals with Disabilities Education Act, this principle holds that all children should have the opportunity to participate in all activities and use all materials in indoor and outdoor spaces.

licensed child care center: A child care company (a for-profit or nonprofit business) that is licensed by the state. These centers provide standardized and regulated care according to state licensing rules.

licensed family child care home: A home care setting that is licensed by the state. These settings adhere to state licensing rules for providing a safe and healthy environment in a home.

macrosystem: A level in Urie Bronfenbrenner's ecological systems theory that includes everything a child encounters, including values, beliefs, customs, culture, and laws.

mathematical awareness: A skill that develops when young children learn to identify, group, and categorize objects; includes number awareness.

mental representation: A mental image of something that is not in a child's view.

mesosystem: A level in Urie Bronfenbrenner's ecological systems theory that includes environments and relationships outside of a child's primary system, such as with school community members and neighbors.

microsystem: A level in Urie Bronfenbrenner's ecological systems theory that includes a child's most immediate environments and relationships, such as those with parents, siblings, teachers, and peers.

mistrust-building sequence: A series of interactions between a child and adult through which mistrust is developed. The sequence begins when a child feels tension and signals a need but the adult does nothing to eliminate the source of tension. The nonresponsive gestures or delayed responses reinforce the child's growing tension and distress, which leads to feelings of mistrust.

myelination: The process by which an axon is encased in myelin. This process begins before birth and continues through adolescence.

myelin sheath: A substance that encases an axon and increases the speed by which information is processed across the axon.

nature influence: The effect of biological factors on an individual.

neural transmitter: A chemical that transfers across a synapse from the axon of one neuron to the dendrites of another neuron.

neuron: A cell that transmits nerve impulses.

nurture influence: The effect of upbringing, health, and environment on an individual.

object permanence: The concept that something out of sight still exists.

older infant: A child between six and twelve months old.

older toddler: A child between twenty-four and thirty-six months old; also called a two-year-old.

perceptual development: A child's increasing ability to perceive the world through his senses. From birth to age three, a child rapidly acquires mastery of his senses by absorbing sensory impressions from everything around him.

personal caregiving philosophy statement: A child care professional's assertion about why she entered the field of early childhood education and how she hopes to deepen her commitment to young children. The statement also covers a caregiver's individual gifts as a provider and her joys and concerns about working with children.

pincer grasp: Forming a circle with the thumb and index finger in order to pick up an object between the two.

plasticity: The brain's ability to change and adapt with ease.

preoperational stage: The second stage in Piaget's theory of cognitive development. A child typically enters this stage at about age two, when she begins to use symbols—including words, features, pictures, and models—to represent objects and events. A child in this stage begins to master reasoning, develops magical beliefs, and shows growing interest in why things happen.

primary care: A best practice recognized in child care. It includes feeding, changing diapers, rocking, soothing, talking, and engaging the child.

primary caregiver: An adult who provides primary, personalized care to a child.

psychosocial theory: Erik Erikson's theory of development, which emphasizes the effect of society and culture on a child's developing sense of self and relationships with others. Erikson's psychosocial theory identifies eight developmental stages, each of which is defined by a unique challenge.

receptive language: A older infant's or toddler's ability to listen to and understand what he hears. Receptive language skills develop before a child can speak with words.

resiliency: The ability to adapt to and survive difficult circumstances. Resiliency requires many social-emotional skills, including a strong sense of self, a personal identity, close relationships with adults and peers, empathy, caring, and the ability to share. Resiliency develops throughout childhood as a child adapts to the changes and challenges of life.

responsive caregiver: An adult who cares for infants, toddlers, and twos; partners with families; ensures secure attachments and relationships between adults and children; and assists children in acquiring skills across the four learning domains.

responsive learning environment: A space that is reassuring, inclusive, and physically safe.

responsive program: A child care setting that is reassuring, inclusive, and physically safe. Behind the scenes, a responsive program is supported by policies and practices that keep spaces—and everyone and everything in them—healthy and safe.

role confusion: The inability to identify one's own personal values and beliefs.

scaffolding: A method of gradually withdrawing assistance as a child constructs her own learning and develops expertise over a task. Scaffolding is an application of Lev Vygotsky's sociocultural theory.

secondary caregiver: An adult who spends considerable time with a child but is not his primary caregiver.

secure attachment: A type of parent-child emotional tie in which a child is content and confident in the presence of her parent. A securely attached child senses that she is safe and provided for when her parent is present. The child seeks the company of her parent only when she needs security, protection, and comfort.

secure relationship: A relationship in which an individual feel safe, respected, valued, and trusted.

self-regulation: A child's ability to control his own emotions and behavior with cognitive methods.

sense of self: A child's awareness of herself in terms of gender roles, racial identity, relationships to others, and so on. Developing a healthy sense of self is an important part of social-emotional development.

sensorimotor stage: The first stage in Piaget's theory of cognitive development. During this stage—from birth to about age two— a child develops cognitive skills through sensory exploration and motor development.

social-emotional development: A child's growing ability to identify, regulate, and express his emotions and to feel concern and empathy for others.

sociocultural theory: A theory developed by Lev Vygotsky about how the environment influences a child's development. His theory is based on the idea that a child's culture deeply influences her beliefs, skills, and customs.

spatial awareness: The ability to understand the position of objects in relation to other objects.

sudden infant death syndrome (SIDS): The unexpected death of a healthy baby who stops breathing during sleep; the cause of SIDS is generally unknown.

symbolic play: A type of play that requires children to make mental representations. Symbolic play creates a foundation for abstract reasoning and more advanced cognitive skills.

synapse: The gap between two nerve cells.

synaptic pruning: The process through which unused neural pathways are stripped away.

tabula rasa: Latin for "blank slate," this term refers to John Locke's theory that a newborn's mind is a blank slate that is filled out by life experiences. Today, this theory is understood to be false.

Touchpoints approach: An approach to caregiving developed by T. Berry Brazelton. This approach identifies key elements found in high-quality early childhood settings, advocates for education and training in child development, and emphasizes continuity of care and positive teacher-child relationships.

trust-building sequence: A series of interactions between a child and adult through which trust is developed. The sequence begins when an infant feels tension and signals need, continues with an adult's response to meet the need, and ends with the infant feeling nurtured and having trust in the adult.

universal design for learning (UDL): Setting up an environment and learning experiences to support every child's learning style and capacity.

vocalization: Any sound that a child makes, which may or may not be actual speech.

young infant: An infant between birth and six months old.

young toddler: A toddler between twelve to twenty-four months old.

zone of proximal development: A term coined by Lev Vygotsky for the period of learning when a child has not yet fully mastered a task but can perform it with help from a member of his culture.

References

Berk, Laura E. 2008. *Infants and Children Prenatal through Middle Childhood*. 6th ed. Boston: Allyn and Bacon.

Brazelton, T. Berry. 2012. "Vision, Mission, Goals." Brazelton Touchpoints Center. Accessed March 9. www.brazeltontouchpoints.org/about/vision.

Brazelton Touchpoints Center. 2007. *A Review of the Early Care and Education Literature: Evidence Base for Touchpoints*. Boston: Brazelton Touchpoints Center.

CAST (Center for Applied Special Technology). 2012. "About UDL." Accessed June 14. www.cast.org/udl/index.html.

CDC (Centers for Disease Control and Prevention). 2012. "Autism Spectrum Disorder (ASDs): Facts about ASDs." Last modified March 29. www.cdc.gov/ncbddd/autism/facts.html.

Churchill, Susan L. 2003. "Goodness-of-Fit in Early Childhood Settings." *Early Childhood Education Journal* 31 (2): 113–18.

Dodge, Diane T., Sherrie Rudick, and Kai-leé Berke. 2006. *Creative Curriculum for Infants, Toddlers and Twos*. 2nd ed. Washington, DC: Teaching Strategies.

Erikson, Erik H. 1963. *Childhood and Society*. New York: W. W. Norton and Company.

Feldman, Robert S. 2007. *Child Development*. 4th ed. Upper Saddle River, NJ: Pearson Education.

First Signs. 2012. "Red Flags." Last modified January 11. www.firstsigns.org/concerns/flags.htm.

Harlow, Harry F. 1958. "The Nature of Love." *American Pyschologist* 13: 573–685.

Harms, Thelma, Debby Cryer, and Richard M. Clifford. 2006. *Infant/Toddler Environment Rating Scale*. Rev. ed. New York: Teachers College Press.

———. 2007. *Family Child Care Environment Rating Scale*. Rev. ed. New York: Teachers College Press.

Kail, Robert V. 2007. *Children and Their Development*. 4th ed. Upper Saddle River, NJ: Prentice Hall.

Meltzoff, Andrew N., and M. Keith Moore. 1997. "Explaining Facial Imitation: A Theoretical Model." *Early Development and Parenting* 6: 179–92.

Mercer, Jean. 2010. "Dr. Stanley Greenspan's Legacy." *Child Myths* (blog), *Psychology Today,* May 2. www.psychologytoday.com/blog/child.

NAEYC (National Association for the Education of Young Children). 2008. *Teacher-Child Ratios within Group Size*. Washington, DC: NAEYC. www.naeyc.org/files/academy/file/Teacher-Child_Ratio_Chart_9_16_08.pdf.

———. 2009. *Where We Stand on Responding to Linguistic and Cultural Diversity*. Washington, DC: NAEYC. www.naeyc.org/files/naeyc/file/positions/diversity.pdf.

———. 2011. "Parent-Teacher Relationships." NAEYC. Accessed January 1. www.naeyc.org/families/PT.

NAEYC and NAECS/SDE (National Association for the Education of Young Children and National Association of Early Childhood Specialists in State Departments of Education). 2003. *Early Childhood Curriculum, Assessment, and Program Evaluation: Building an Effective Accountable System in Programs for Children Birth through Age 8*. Washington, DC: NAEYC. www.naeyc.org/files/naeyc/file/positions/pscape.pdf.

NICHD (National Institute of Child Health and Human Development). 2005. "Safe Sleep for Your Baby: Reduce the Risk of Sudden Infant Death Syndrome (SIDS)." Last modified August 13, 2009. www.nichd.nih.gov/publications/pubs/safe_sleep_gen.cfm.

Olds, Anita. 2001. *Child Care Design Guide*. New York: McGraw-Hill.

Patterson, Charlotte J. 2009. *Infancy and Childhood*. New York: McGraw-Hill.

Piaget, Jean. 1973. *The Child and Reality: Problems of Genetic Psychology*. New York: Grossman Publishers.

PITC (Program for Infant/Toddler Care). 2012. "PITC's Six Program Policies." Accessed June 11. www.pitc.org/pub/pitc_docs/about.html.

PBS (Public Broadcasting Service). 2011. "Early Learning: Speaking Parentese." PBS Parents. Accessed June 27. www.pbs.org/parents/earlylearning/parentese.html.

Singer, Jayne. 2007. "The Brazelton Touchpoints Approach to Infants and Toddlers in Care: Foundation for a Lifetime of Learning and Loving." *Dimensions of Early Childhood* 35 (3): 4–10.

Thomas, Alexander, Stella Chess, and Herbert G. Birch. 1970. "The Origin of Personality." *Scientific American* 223 (2): 102–9.

Index